Linda Clark's
REJUVENATION
PROGRAMME

Linda Clark reports on the most recent information about methods to restore and maintain vigour and mental alertness into advancing old age. She suggests that ageing is really prolonged neglect of the body over the years and that, with the right food supplements, digestive aids and mental attitude, this process can actually be reversed.

By the same author
HANDBOOK OF NATURAL REMEDIES FOR
  COMMON AILMENTS

Linda Clark's
REJUVENATION PROGRAMME

For reversing the ageing process

by
LINDA CLARK

THORSONS PUBLISHERS LIMITED
Wellingborough, Northamptonshire

First published in the United Kingdom 1980
This Edition first published 1985

*Original American edition published by
The Devin-Adair Company, Old Greenwich,
Connecticut, USA.*

© LINDA CLARK 1979

*This book is sold subject to the condition that it shall not, by way of trade or otherwise,
be lent, re-sold, hired out, or otherwise circulated without the publisher's prior consent
in any form of binding or cover other than that in which it is published and without
a similar condition including this condition being imposed on the subsequent purchaser.*

British Library Cataloguing in Publication Data

Clark, Linda
    Linda Clark's rejuvenation programme. —
(Nature's way)
1. Rejuvenation
I. Title   II. Series
613   QP90

ISBN 0-7225-1149-3

Printed in Great Britain by
Richard Clay (The Chaucer Press) Ltd,
Bungay, Suffolk

Contents

Chapter		Page
1.	Ageing Can be Pleasant	7
2.	Why Your Body Needs Help	13
3.	The Effect of Cells on Rejuvenation	16
4.	Wake Up Your Glands	20
5.	New v. Old Medical Treatment	23
6.	What to Do About Degenerative Diseases	27
7.	Enzymes for Health and Youth	36
8.	Other Foods for Rejuvenation	43
9.	Beginning Your Rejuvenation Programme	45
10.	Rejuvenation Therapy	53
11.	Power Foods	62
12.	Other Aids to Rejuvenation	72
13.	Regular Exercise Can Rejuvenate You	80
14.	Breathing for Health	91
15.	Changing Your Life Through Thought	96
16.	Advice for Special Senior Problems	102
17.	Your Rejuvenation Blueprint	113
18.	Rejuvenation from Tibet	116
	Suggested Reading	124
	Index	126

1

Ageing Can be Pleasant

This morning I received a phone call from one of my daughters. She lives in New York, I live in California. She apologized when I answered the phone. 'I'm sorry to bother you with a problem, Mom,' she began, 'But I am at my wits' end with one of my teenage children. I need suggestions and advice.' She then outlined the problem.

I felt flattered to receive this call because most younger parents these days are contemptuous about advice from their elders. They want to do things *their* way without any interference from the older generation, who are too often considered old fogies. Believe me, I have learned the hard way, that it is not wise to offer advice unless it is asked for, otherwise it will be rejected. But in this case it was asked for, and since my daughter knew I had at one time been a teenage counsellor as well as a parent, she hoped I would know the solution. Fortunately, I had an answer that satisfied her and relieved her worry.

Before this phone call I had already been at work on this book, inspired by my discovery that the older generation has become a forgotten species. Whereas in their younger years they were active, admired by others, fresh and vital in appearance, as the years have rolled by these same people find that they are becoming 'has-beens', too often ignored, and left on the shelf in loneliness or illness and with nothing pleasant to look forward to.

Most of us seniors, of which I am now one, have had our heyday. As an international lecturer and writer I have had my share of attention on the platform, radio, and television. I have been a consultant, as I explained, to teenagers, and later to middle-agers. One day not too long ago I was with my second daughter when we met a stranger who knew nothing about either of us. The not-too-young stranger, a man, could not take his eyes off my daughter, who is admittedly attractive, while he ignored me completely. So I know how it feels. Please understand: I did not begrudge the attention to my daughter, but I did begrudge the fact that the newcomer did not even acknowledge that I existed.

I suddenly realized what a Senior has to face. Many are considered burdens by their children who do not know what to do with them. Retirement homes or centres are a help, but even they can be depressing because of so many old, decrepit people present, leaning on canes, walking on crutches, or pushing about in wheelchairs. And the average nursing home is usually worse.

Some people, as they get older, are in better condition than others. We have all seen pictures in the newspapers of centenarians or couples who have celebrated their fiftieth or sixtieth anniversary. And they look it! You think, 'But for the grace of God, there go I!' But others at late ages are alert, vital, healthy, and really enjoying life. I know a counsellor in her eighties who never forgets anything, is in constant demand by people all over the nation. Her phone is never idle. Another couple, about ninety, a retired doctor and his wife (he has long been interested in reversing ageing), have a ten-acre holding they supervise, and they love every minute of it. Others are adored by their children and friends and are sought after, admired, and respected by people of various ages.

There are people in different parts of the world who live to, and well beyond, the hundred-year mark, enjoying good vision, hearing, health, and tremendous endurance all the way. Men at this late age even beget children. These Seniors are in far better condition than some of our forty- and fifty-year-olds. They are also respected for their wisdom, consulted by their juniors, and, in short, lead happy, useful lives.[1] This is as it should be.

Several researchers in the field of gerontology (fancy name for the study of ageing) insist that the human body, if treated right, is good for at least a hundred years of active, enjoyable, healthy life. So being older does not necessarily mean we need be decrepit.

The Need to be Needed

The stigma of mandatory retirement at sixty-five is limiting to the individual and to society. For too long public policy has been influenced by a person's years rather than by ability. The woman counsellor or previously mentioned, who is extremely successful and praised for her helpful services to clients, told me recently that although she is in her eighties, she dare not say so or her clients would lose confidence in her because of her age and she might lose her job. This is absurd.

Age sixty-five, and beyond, should not be the end of life, but, as with those in their forties and fifties, just the beginning!

Meanwhile, too many identify ageing with wrinkles, a tottery gait, and general disability. This need not be so either. Instead of cringing as we get older, we should learn how to rehabilitate ourselves so that we can be proud to be good examples of an age at which we have earned the respect of everyone.

So the number of years one lives should not be the criterion of ability during so-called ageing. If we make it so, it is our own fault. We should refuse to give in to the ageing process and should begin to do something constructive about it so that we get better as we get older, not worse.

We all want to be needed, loved, and respected by others instead of being shelved. That is why I was flattered to receive the phone call from my daughter mentioned at the beginning.

For many months I have been searching widely for methods of rehabilitation or prevention of so-called ageing problems. I have tried them all personally, and those that have proved successful in personal improvement I will share with you in this book.

Positive Attitude

To begin with, I do not like to be called a 'senior citizen' or, even worse, 'elderly'. Such pity-evoking terms are but further stigmas. I prefer the term 'Senior'. Seniors in school are looked up to, so why not Seniors in life? So let's begin our rehabilitation by using this term. Don't think of yourself as elderly or a senior citizen, but as a respected *Senior*. In fact, do not tell your age at all unless you want to or have to.

Some people advertise their advancing years with pride, hoping to attract sympathy or hoping that people will exclaim, 'Surely you can't be *that* old!' I know one ninety-four-year-old woman who looks closer to the average sixty-four. She is slim, trim, attractive, chic, and well groomed. She has good eyesight, good hearing, good health, and is mentally alert. She is incredible, but not vain about it, accepting her condition as her due. She never tells her age. Her relatives are the ones who are proud of her.

However, most Seniors have allowed themselves to become decrepit and no one wants to be around them. I believe we must reverse the trend so that younger people will really want to be with us. But we must work to improve ourselves and earn respect from others. Having finally become a Senior myself, I realize that most Seniors need counselling the same as teenagers and middle-agers. And so I decided I want to help bring credit to our group. I hope you will join me.

Constructive Action

Instead of becoming glued to television or a rocking chair, we should begin by doing something constructive. One good start is to be of service to others, *any* service you can find. If you have certain knowledge at your disposal, dust it off and put it to use. If not, learn something new. Higher education is readily available and there are adult courses for those who want to earn a degree without leaving their area, or who are giving up other activities, even jobs, for additional learning denied earlier.

Many women who had to cut short their education due to marriage and having children now have a chance to complete their studies. Others are seeking, and getting, instruction for a new career or an enriched retirement.

You may say that you don't feel well enough to take up a new interest. This is a common complaint of Seniors and as such is the main subject of this book: *How to feel better as well as look better. It can be done.* But, again, no one but *you* can do it. Now is the time for you to get busy so that you will be ready for anything you would really like to do, yet hesitate to attempt because of your present condition. It is not necessary to sit around waiting for the grim reaper!

Conquering the Fear of Death

If you fear death, this too can be overcome. Some metaphysicians tell us that we die only when we are ready to die, not before, no matter what the circumstance of death. One man was killed by a falling tree. This was no accident (metaphysicians and parapsychologists do not believe there are 'accidents'). The explanation given was that the man was ready to die and walked under the tree of his own volition when it was ready to fall. Some go still further. They insist that we choose our time to be born, our parents, our birthplace and date, and the type of life we are to lead in order to learn the lessons we need to learn. I am not urging you to believe this, merely suggesting that there are those who have studied the subject in depth to learn that we have been given a free will to do whatever we wish. According to this philosophy, you make your own life and cannot blame circumstances, your parents, your children, or anyone else for the results. Remember this point, since it bears on what kind of life you can build for yourself so that you *will* like it!

Some people do not fear death as much as the moment of dying, which they believe involves great pain. We are told that this is not necessarily so: The spirit, or soul, is apparently lifted free of the body before actual death takes place. The impact of a car, plane, or other accident is not felt.

How do we know this? Because some people have died, and returned to tell us about the experience. Surprisingly, these reports agree. There are stories galore of people who have 'died' on the operating table or by other means. The returnee has stated that life on the other side is beautiful, painless, and like walking into 'God's other room', filled with beautiful flowers, music, scenery, as well as friends, relatives, and other loved ones, even pets, who have preceded them. The reason they returned, they stated, is that they were sent back because their job here was not yet finished or someone needed them. They did return, but because of the experience they lost all fear of death once and for all.

Dr Elisabeth Kübler-Ross, formerly a country doctor in Switzerland, now a Chicago psychiatrist and author and lecturer, specializes in helping people conquer the fear of dying. In an interview published in the *San Francisco Chronicle* she told of her research, which has convinced her that 'beyond a shadow of a doubt' there is life after death. She tells of accident victims doctors thought had died, but who later revived. These patients said they had a feeling of departing from their physical bodies and floating blissfully above them, even hearing everything said by the doctors and nurses, which was later confirmed.

Dr Kübler-Ross tells of a two-year-old boy who apparently died, but was later saved by doctors. He told his mother he was dead and it was so beautiful where he went that he did not want to come back; he added that he was with Mary and Jesus. But Mary told him he must go back to help his mother.

So, rather than spending time and energy worrying about dying, you can postpone the date of dying and spend the same time and energy in making your life pleasant until you are ready to go. Since you have been given a free will, you can use it for good or bad, happiness or sadness. You can be the person you want to be. You can be vital, flexible, healthy, attractive, alert, and happy *at any age*. You can programme such a life and make it yours!

Or, if you insist, you can do the opposite. You can be negative, complaining, critical, full of self-pity and unhappiness, attracting negative people and conditions into your life. Nobody will stop you if that's what you want.

Your life is what you make it. You, and you alone, are the pilot, and you can compute how you are going to spend the remaining years of your life. You have heard the statement: 'Today is the beginning of the rest of your life.' You need not live in the past, repeating to bored listeners what has already happened to you. You can embark on a new life and a happy, healthy existence.

It can be done. It has been done. This book will tell you how to do it. Be prepared for some fascinating surprises to help you on your way!

REFERENCES
(See *Bibliography* for fuller details)

1. Luigi Cornaro, *How to Live 100 Years*.

2

Why Your Body Needs Help

We take our bodies and health for granted – at first. As long as they work reasonably well and don't give us any trouble, we pay little attention to them. But when they begin to complain and stop working properly, with small disturbances like headaches and constant colds and later more serious ailments, then we panic and are ready to stop the neglect and do something about it. We have had a rude awakening to the fact our bodies and health are not necessarily automatic.

When we were born, we didn't realize what a gold mine we had. Unless during pregnancy our mother took drugs, smoked excessively, was an alcoholic, or did not eat right, we were probably born with good health and all the necessary parts. Otherwise we may have been marked at birth with a defect or diseased condition. Some babies, born of alcoholic mothers, actually come into this world with alcohol on their breath like a drunken adult. Or if the nutrition of the mother lacked a certain vitamin at a specific time during pregnancy, the child could be born with a cleft palate. This has been definitely established in many cases.

Even heart defects, eyes that need glasses early in life, and a host of other 'inherited' weaknesses are often due to the fact that the mother did not eat the right food during pregnancy to provide her child with the correct building material. If she added drugs or other poisons, the baby paid additionally for it throughout its lifetime.

Diet and Inherited Health

What about the statement that to be in good health we should choose our ancestors? This can be true because of our genes, those mysterious inborn influences that affect our bodies, our appearance, our behaviour, and our health. These genes may be inherited from our parents, grandparents, and great-grandparents. Not only do different families have certain genes; certain nationalities do too. Orientals can eat and thrive on food Westerners may or may not thrive on. Italians, Norwegians, and other nationalities, ditto. This does not mean that we cannot enjoy Oriental or Italian food occasionally. But for a steady diet the people of one country may not thrive on the full-time diet of another country. For example, the amount of protein available for one country may not satisfy the needs of another. The Norwegians thrive on fish, which is plentiful in that area. The Italians for the most part keep their figures eating pasta every day. Various peoples have been conditioned for centuries by the genes of their own nationality. The body does not welcome sudden, sharp changes, and it may take a generation or more to adjust to such changes.

Our glands, the machines that run our bodies, are also affected by our ancestors. If they ate good, wholesome food, this served as good 'fuel' for their glands, which were passed on to their children and their successors. But if the good fuel was not constantly supplied, the glands of one generation could fail to protect them, or the next generation.

I have already told the story elsewhere of four children, a sister and three brothers, who lived to ripe old ages with surprisingly good health in spite of a poor diet. On searching further, I learned that the parents of these four children lived on a farm, as did their parents, and *their* parents. Their food was nutritious, their health was good. Glands were sustained by wholesome farm food, and health was evident in each generation – up until the final one, the woman and her three brothers. *They had moved to a city and eaten city food.* Even so, they lived to an incredibly advanced age until suddenly, one by one, each of them 'fell apart' and died. It was similar to a house that looks sound on the outside, then one day collapses from termites that have been riddling the inside of the structure. The poor city diet had caught up with this family. Good glands could not be perpetuated without proper fuel, so they finally gave out.

Respecting Your Body

When we are born, let us hope with a healthy body, we have a possession money cannot buy. Our parents, if they are wise, take care of our bodies for us until we are old enough and presumably wise enough to assume that responsibility. But at this point most people begin to deteriorate without realizing it. They eat what tastes good, ignoring whether or not it is good for them. They begin to smoke, drink, and take drugs because it is the 'thing' to do. They lose sleep, burn the candle at both ends, and resent it if anyone tells them not to. They start gaining weight on junk food and then try to take it off with a fad diet that leaves their bodies even more nutritionally exhausted. They begin to develop aches and pains, and rush to the nearest doctor to patch them up with drugs. Unfortunately, drugs do not cure; they merely give temporary relief, as, for example, an aspirin may stop a headache but it does not remove the cause.

So not until the body starts to scream do we become scared. The aches and pains are the forerunners of old age. Yet if you warn young people to stop taking their most precious assets – their body and health – for granted and urge them to start treating these assets with respect, they rebel at 'authority'. You probably did the same thing yourself. We all learn the hard way, or else we do not know what to do the right way.

Dr José Froimovich, a distinguished gerontologist from Chile, who has devoted over thirty-five years to the study of the causes of ageing, says: 'Deterioration of our body is a result of increasing deficiencies within the body's tissue. Yet such conditions can be changed.' He continues: 'Why should we accept as an unchangeable fact of life that our body should start to give out just when life's experience enables our brain to function at its best? This very period in our life is the most valuable age for the human in society.'

Fortunately, it is possible to reprogramme our glands and to reverse many of these ageing symptoms, if you know how. And that is what this book is about.

You will find many hints in this book. You may not be able to follow them all. If you cannot, there is no need to feel guilty. Make note of those that appeal to you as you read the book.

3

The Effect of Cells on Rejuvenation

Our bodies are made of cells, or to turn it around, cells help make our bodies. They occur in all tissues, including the skin, every muscle, every gland, every organ. They are the foundation of the body structure. I am not punning when I say never sell a cell short. Nurture your cells, encourage them, pamper them, and you will be paid back in full with accrued interest.

Because your cells are the fabric from which your body is woven, with proper care you can help your cells prevent your body from wearing out prematurely. When your car wears out, you must buy a new one. When your body wears out, you cannot buy a new one, but you can help your cells rehabilitate the body you already have.

There are about sixty trillion cells in the body, a number impossible to visualize. They age at different rates in different ways. But the slowdown of the creation of new cells is the basis of ageing. This cell loss is greater in the glands, nerves, muscles, and kidneys. Cell loss can also be due at any age to poisons in the environment, such as air pollution, or to alcohol, smoking, radiation, even some food additives. Certain vitamins (C and E) can help protect the cells from such disturbances.

Cells are constantly dying and being replaced with new cells. In early youth newly formed cells outnumber the dying cells. In middle age the number of dying cells is balanced by equivalent new cells. In ageing the old cells may die faster than they can be replaced by new cells. Old cells divide to form new cells, but old cells that have gone through many divisions are less efficient in division and rebirth. Some scientists believe that certain cells, such as brain cells, do not divide at all. So we must protect the cells we already have.

Cell Reproduction Research

Hans J. Kugler, Ph.D., the author of a book on slowing down the ageing process, states: 'It is therefore of the most importance to supply our cells with optimum conditions *at all times* in order to keep them alive for the longest time possible.'

The body is said to renew itself completely every seven years, but the quality of the new cells can be no better, as the cell manufacture continues, than the material, or food, on which they are fed. If the cells are allowed to deteriorate, they may reproduce inferior offspring – cells of poor quality, which in turn are perpetuated. As you can see, this creates second-, third-, or fourth-class cells incapable of keeping the body functioning at top performance.

But there is still hope when this happens. Other scientists have learned that at certain stages, if only 10 per cent of the cells are in good condition, with the proper help those cells can eventually regenerate the entire body. Cell reproduction in early youth is rapid and automatic, whereas it may take longer for cells to regenerate toward the later years in life. So we cannot leave it to chance; we must work at it!

Even so, there is proof that, given the proper conditions, cells can multiply faster than usual. In the Department of Molecular, Cellular, and Developmental Biology, University of Colorado, researchers found that cells growing in laboratory flasks could be reconstructed within a span of several hours. The researchers found that they could take cells apart and put them together again in better combinations than before. This discovery surprised even the team of scientists who accomplished this feat. In 1975 two research physiologists at the University of California, Drs Lester Packer and James R. Smith, found that by raising the oxygen level in cells and exposing the cells to visible light, the treated cells continued to grow and reproduce beyond the 120-division point, comparable to more than double their usual life span.

And there is still earlier proof in a well-known example. In 1912 Dr Alexis Carrel initiated an experiment at the Rockefeller Institute for Medical Research in New York. He placed a fraction of heart muscle in a nutrient medium, and this piece of heart muscle lived for over thirty years, at which time the experiment was discontinued. Dr Carrel received a Nobel Prize for his achievement. *But certain nutrients were needed to feed and nourish the heart muscle in order to keep it alive and well.*

Other similar, more recent, experiments are in progress. As proof, at Lawrence Berkeley Laboratory, cells assumed to reproduce only fifty times divided 120 times, and are still dividing. Vitamin E is used as a nutrient, and the cells appear young and healthy. But additional nutrients are also needed.

Nutrition and Rehabilitation

Dr José Froimovich, mentioned in the previous chapter, has supplied certain nutrients to scores of ageing men and women and has produced amazing results in their rehabilitation, about which more later. It is interesting to note at this point that Dr Froimovich believes we are not living to our full age potential of 100 to 120 years. Yet there are scores of examples of members of various groups in Europe and elsewhere who do live that long and in good health, as we have already learned. But in these cases certain requirements have been fulfilled for them during their entire lives. One of the requirements appears to be correct food; another, sufficient oxygen. Both are needed for optimum health and survival of the cells.

Man cannot live without oxygen. We can live for some time without food, less time without water, but we can survive only a few minutes without oxygen. Normally we get our oxygen from the air. Today, unfortunately, because of air pollution the oxygen supply is affected, interfering with the amount delivered to the cells of those who breathe contaminated air.

Even if the body takes in sufficient air, in some people the oxygen necessary to sustain certain parts of the body cannot adequately reach these areas to provide proper nourishment, and the cells suffer. This is especially true of the brain, eyes, ears, and heart, which can become oxygen-starved, resulting in malfunction. Have you noticed how many people suffer from fuzzy thinking? They start to tell you something, perhaps about somebody, and cannot remember the point or recall the name of the person. Put it down to too little oxygen supply! It is becoming a common occurrence for all ages.

Fortunately, there are methods of providing oxygen and proper nourishment not only to stimulate cells and glands, but

THE EFFECT OF CELLS ON REJUVENATION

also to remove waste products, thus renewing both cells and glandular functions. This, in turn, helps to slow down or reverse the ageing process and encourages the body to rehabilitate itself. This is a new and exciting concept, and I will tell you how to do it in a later chapter.

In some hospitals there are now oxygen machines for outpatients. The wife of one man, who was depressed and could not remember anything well, told me that after a short treatment by one of these machines the temporary change in his behaviour and mental acuity was almost unbelievable. Someone else has suggested that the time may come (if air contamination continues) when we may rent or buy an oxygen machine for home use to provide us with a dose when we need it. Other, easier methods of increasing our oxygen supply will be discussed subsequently.

Certain nutrients can stimulate the oxygen supply in various cells of the body. This should not be confused with cell therapy discussed in Chapter 10, by which fresh animal cells are injected into waning bodies. People I have talked to who have had this therapy have mixed feelings about the results. In some cases, they report, the process did provide temporary vitality, in some instances more, in others less, but the effect often was of limited duration. Apparently cell nutrients are needed on a *continuous basis*. This you can achieve in your own home.

But this places the responsibility fully upon your own shoulders. You, all on your own, can help control your health and prevent rapid ageing. No one else can do it for you. Your life is in your own hands, and it is never too late to begin to attain improvement. The sooner you start, the earlier the results.

4

Wake Up Your Glands

The glands in your body are some of the most important machinery you own. They control vital functions that influence your health as well as the rate of ageing. For years prophets of doom have been warning us that after the age of forty our glands begin to slow down, and there is nothing we can do about it.

If this is so, why is it that there are those, regardless of age, who are as mentally alert as a much younger person? Why is it that in some parts of the world men and women live to the ripe age of a hundred and beyond? Why is it that men at this late date have retained their sexual potency and even sired children? It is undoubtedly because the glands of these people are still in good working order. If some people can keep their glands in good condition, why not you?

Glands, as well as cells, need proper fuel, which is absolutely essential to keep them in good condition. It is no doubt true that genes (which you inherit from your ancestors) also play a part. But how did your ancestors' glands become so superior? Their way of life, as well as proper fuel, had a decided effect. Even if you have inherited or developed poor glands, researchers say they can be improved. The proper fuel (nutrition), plus exercise, plus the right mental attitude can combine to help bring about this improvement.

Undermining the Glands

In younger years glands and cells seem to function almost automatically. Youngsters usually do not give it all a second thought. They appear to have inexhaustible energy and usually look well regardless of what they eat or do. However, if they live on junk food, dissipate, ignore sleep, good hygiene, exercise, and other body-caring measures, little by little their glandular machinery is sabotaged. A kind of time bomb slowly builds up at the continual use of poor fuel, drugs, alcohol, smoking, and other such indignities undermines the health and strength of the precious glands. Toxins accumulate in the body, and your once seemingly foolproof body or machine now suddenly develops knocks, creaks, and groans. With alarm you begin to think, 'I'm getting old!'

There is nothing inexplicable or even sudden about what has happened. Your gradual mistreatment of your body has been going on for a long time until finally the time bomb does explode. But this, of all times, is not the moment to give up. Instead, you will have to switch the control from automatic to manual and take over your own programming. This is the moment to get busy.

A New Way of Life

I am told by people who work in nursing and retirement homes that many who live there have given up and lost the will to live. They are anxious to die and get the misery over with. Otherwise they might not be there at all. If they were full of pep, enjoying life, attractive to others, no one would force them, or even want them, to be there. In the East, older men and women are respected for their wisdom and other assets. They remain with their families, who love and enjoy them and want them in their home circle as long as they live.

But since you yourself have produced this condition of so-called 'ageing,' which is actually little more than prolonged neglect, you can also dig yourself out and pull yourself up by your own bootstraps. The information on how to do it is fascinating and included in this book. Roll up your sleeves and get to work. You will find information to help you look better within minutes. You will find information to help you feel better and more energetic within a few short months. But *this means adopting a completely new way of life from now on.* Once you decide to rehabilitate yourself, you must not turn back. Is it worth the effort? You bet it is. You will not only find something to live for, but this new way of life will help you to enjoy life more than ever before.

A programme to get you started on your way will show you,

first, what to eat, later, how to exercise pleasantly and easily, and still later, how to think your way to rejuvenation.

Others have accomplished wonders. So can you.

Tips for Success

1. Get a large notebook, or use the empty pages at the back of this book. Write down the items you wish to incorporate in your programmes as you read about them or think of them. You may have to adjust the programme to your own needs.

2. Read what you have written every day so you will not forget.

3. *Do not talk about this programme to others.* Otherwise they may try to discourage you. Remember that when someone announces embarking on a slimming diet, for some reason almost everyone tries to interfere and tempt the would-be reducer to abandon the programme. So do not talk about this programme, just do it quietly and firmly.

4. You may, at first, notice only a good day now and then. These occasional good days may be followed by one or more bad days. The reason? The body does not like change. It likes the old routine, the old comfort. But this programme will have to be *a new way of life*. As you are consistent, eventually the good days will outnumber the bad days. One expert who has observed the effects of this programme on many people says it usually takes from one to three months (depending on how far gone you were when you started) before you realize you are feeling good. Whatever happens, *don't give up*. Eventually, first one reward, then another will become evident.

5. There is no quick panacea, no magic wand, no single secret (except determination and work) to produce a miracle when your back is turned. Results come from an applied programme of combined approaches, both mental and physical.

Are you ready? If so, I am ready to turn over the keys to you. Good luck.

5

New v. Old Medical Treatment

It may be true that *some* people are staying young longer, are healthier than usual in later age, but these people are exceptions. Either their genes are special, or they have learned what to do to help themselves, as this book is intended to help *you*.

There are basically two types of disease: infectious and degenerative. Infectious diseases are those that are usually contagious and are transmitted by a 'germ' from other people, food, water, air, insects, soil, and other sources. A cold, flu, smallpox, malaria, amoebic dysentery, even tuberculosis are all considered infectious diseases. Infectious disease *may* respond to a drug, depending on the disease, but the drug must be chosen carefully by the doctor, since some drugs produce side effects worse than the disease itself. In a life-or-death matter an antibiotic or so-called 'miracle drug' may indeed save a life. But these drugs should not be used indiscriminately or continued indefinitely. For routine ailments there are safer and wiser treatments.

Natural Remedies

I recently learned of two doctors who found this out for themselves. One doctor was caught in a blizzard on a house call to the back country, where, abandoning his car, he nearly collapsed as he was forced to reach safety on foot. He fell, breaking several ribs, and was rescued by a farmer's family, who gave him not only shelter but every type of home care: good food, a comfortable bed, and tender loving attention. Since his 'black bag' had been left behind in his car, there were no drugs available. He gave his rescuers instructions for strapping his ribs correctly. There was nothing else to do but wait for the snow-plough to get through and bring medical help. This took nearly two weeks while the doctor was recuperating from shock, stress, and pain.

Eventually another doctor arrived, complete with drugs. But the injured doctor refused the drugs. He said to the surprised visiting doctor: 'I am astonished how, without any drugs at all, I have been getting well anyway. I have given this much thought and have decided I have been overdoing drugs with my patients. I am going to stop it!'

Let's face it, Nature knows better than man. There are other types of healing remedies that are more natural and effective and safer than drugs. For example, vitamin C, if used in proper amounts, has cured infections after a drug has proved useless. Homoeopathy is another type of medical treatment elected by a few doctors after they have completed their medical school training. Many homoeopathic physicians have become so amazed at the quick, easy, and effective recoveries from a myriad of diseases that they have largely given up the use of drugs. The tiny homoeopathic tablets, used for centuries with safety, are chosen with great care for the *person*, not the *disease*, and have produced miracle after miracle in healing when drugs have failed. Orthodox doctors condemn them as 'folly', even though the doctors who use homoeopathy have had the same initial medical training and have merely added homoeopathy as an extra elective upon their graduation.[1] Many orthodox doctors, who do not understand this type of treatment, laugh at it. They also laugh at nutrition for the same reason.

Yet some open-minded doctors are beginning to study and use not only homoeopathy, but such alternative therapies as nutrition, herbs, acupuncture or acupressure (without needles), even spiritual healing, with remarkable success. And the nutritional approach to disease is sweeping the world as a result of patients who have tried these safer, simpler remedies with astonishing results.

It is heartwarming that some doctors are beginning to turn to these more natural methods, alternatives to routine use of drugs. A recent convention called 'The Physician of the Future' was attended by seventy-two doctors. The event, featuring such alternatives, proved so successful that it was repeated the following year with 2,500 doctors present! The programme also included the study of nutrition (vitamins and minerals, etc.), which doctors are not taught in medical schools, but which patients are demanding. As a result, many flexible doctors are beginning to study and learn on their own this logical nutritional method of helping their patients. An era of medical freedom is apparently in sight.

Degenerative Diseases

Degenerative diseases are a different problem altogether from infectious diseases. These include cardiovascular disease, arteriosclerosis or atherosclerosis, high blood pressure, diabetes, hypoglycemia, kidney diseases, some types of arthritis, and others. Such diseases involve a breakdown of body cells, eventually leading to the degeneration of the body itself. Drugs may temporarily remove some of the *symptoms*, but do not remove the cause. We have noted how aspirin stops a headache, but does not remove the underlying cause. Scientists and some doctors are just beginning to realize that a degenerative disturbance or disease can actually be due to undernutrition, causing the breakdown of the cells that have not been fed properly and leading to various degenerative diseases in various people, depending upon individual weaknesses. As proof, many times these degenerative conditions have been reversed by restoring the deficiency through proper nutrition.

Meanwhile, a great many orthodox doctors refuse to accept this concept, since they were taught about drugs only. They really believe that the nutritional approach is fraudulent. An example of this comes to mind. Recently, after finding that natural food fibre in the diet (rather than bland, unnatural foods) could prevent many intestinal ailments, including cancer, doctors the world over were electrified at the news. The physicians who had made the discovery took X-rays and photographs of African natives on both types of diet and showed these pictures to international medical groups. A doctor in one group that viewed these convincing pictures was heard to say, 'I cannot believe my eyes that anything you put in your mouth could improve your health.'

This shocking statement indicates that the lack of

nutritional instruction in medical school amounts to brainwashing. As another example, at a hearing against a nutritional M.D. who has been getting people well by nutrition instead of drugs, and therefore provoking the wrath of the orthodox medics, who persecuted him and took away his licence, it became clear that the accusing orthodox doctors present actually sincerely believed that nutrition as medicine is a fraud. Even transplants of heart, kidney, and other organs (with a high death rate) are being used instead of the easier, safer, painless, and natural remedies. Again we come to the superiority of nature as compared with the ineffectuality of man. For instance, everyone has heard of patients who have received a clean bill of health following a medical checkup and who died from a heart attack within days or weeks.

In the case of degenerative disease, feeding the cells and glands what they need has helped many to become and remain stronger, thus preventing (or reversing) degeneration. This method has even benefited some infectious diseases through prevention, since proper nutrition can help the body build more resistance to both bacterial and viral invasions.

In the next chapter you will see how nutrition can be an important factor in conquering degenerative diseases that, to date, have been considered killers. Be prepared for some encouraging surprises. This method provides great hope.

REFERENCES
(See *Bibliography* for fuller details)

1. Due to orthodox pressures very few homoeopaths are available. For further details write to: The British Homoeopathic Association, 27a Devonshire Street, London WIN 1RJ

6

What to Do About Degenerative Diseases

Many Seniors as they become older, worry about the degenerative diseases from which so many of their friends or relatives die, especially heart attacks and strokes. Most of these premature deaths can be prevented by the newer, natural treatment: nutrition. Countless couples in their later years have been broken up by deaths from these ailments, leaving grieving widows or widowers to finish their lives alone. Treatments are now available to help prevent such unnecessary loss.

Furthermore, these treatments, tested and recommended by enlightened doctors, can usually be used at home. Since there is a saying, 'You are as young as your arteries,' which some people believe to be true, let us begin with arteries and how you can improve them.

Artery Problems
Artery problems are usually classified as *arterio*-sclerosis, and *athero*sclerosis. Their meaning differs slightly. *Arterio*sclerosis, often called hardening of the arteries, is actually a thickening and narrowing of the artery walls. *Athero*sclerosis, on the other hand, is a filling up or clogging of the arteries. As the clogging increases, the amount of blood that can be pumped through them diminishes, and various parts of the body, including the brain, eyes, arms, legs, or heart, may be cut off from their necessary blood supply, leading to strokes or heart attacks. Some people suffer from artery problems that are less serious, at least at first. So it is important to prevent or reverse this constriction of body flow to all parts of the body. The Longevity Research Institute of Santa Barbara, California, reports: 'Deposits in the arteries are called plaques, and these

accumulate, perhaps leading to a complete block in the artery, or breaking into fragments. These fragments may be carried away in the bloodstream only to block another smaller artery some place downstream. ... To live and do its job, each of the body's millions of cells needs to have nutrients brought to it by the blood supply ... to keep the body cells alive and healthy, the arteries have to remain open and unclogged. If some of the arteries become clogged ... the body cells served by those arteries will die *for lack of oxygen and other nutrients*' (emphasis added).

Too many people have artery problems without realizing it. But how can they avoid or reverse the condition? The treatment is twofold: (1) to provide the body with the correct nutrients to keep the cells healthy, as well as to dissolve the accumulations already present (this can be done and has been done); (2) to supply oxygen to the body cells for additional insurance and health. Natural, do-it-yourself techniques, discussed later, are available.

The Longevity Research Institute

Orthodox physicians often resort to bypass surgery and drugs for artery problems. But the Longevity Research Institute (L.R.I.) has developed an alternative to these extreme therapies: They use a preventive programme that consists mainly of a low-fat, low-cholesterol diet, plus exercise. To give this group due credit, this is definitely a step forward, at least compared to surgery and drugs; and by means of this programme, the Institute has had some remarkable cases of patient improvement.

As an example, one woman had been treated for angina at age sixty-seven; for a severe heart attack at seventy-five; and still later, at eighty-one, for congestive heart failure, hypertension, angina, intermittent claudication, arthritis, and atherosclerosis. Finally she was placed on the Institute's programme and, subsequently, won two gold medals in the 1974 California Senior Olympics. At eighty-five she has won four gold medals, runs a mile and a half daily, plus riding ten to fifteen miles on a stationary bicycle. She also does workouts at a gymnasium twice weekly.

This L.R.I. Programme, which features the use of exercise, not only severely restricts cholesterol foods and fats, even many natural ones, but it also restricts vitamin/mineral supplements, considered so important by other researchers, who recommend these and other measures in addition to exercise with encouraging results.

What Clogs Arteries?

In order to understand how you can unclog your arteries through natural methods it is necessary to understand what clogs them. The deposits in the arteries have been found to be made up of fats, cholesterol, and sometimes calcium. Orthodox doctors assume that these substances *must* be present because they are taken in through the diet. Hence they warn their patients to stop eating cholesterol foods, such as organ meats (liver, sweetbreads, brains), even eggs and avocados, although these foods have some of the highest concentrations of vitamins, minerals, and hormones, all needed by the body and cells for health.

Nutritionists have denied for years that eggs and nutritious organ foods are dangerous. Now there is new, convincing evidence that they are right, and that there is a better way of handling the artery problem.

Research shows that cholesterol is needed by the glands, including the sex glands, and if there is not enough of this substance available, the body manufactures it whether we eat it or not! In fact, a recent researcher stated that if we deny the body cholesterol in the form of foods, it works much more furiously to manufacture *more* cholesterol. So it appears that those who exclude these substances from the diet may be barking up a wrong tree.

Richard A. Passwater, whose specialties include the study of arteries as well as the subject of ageing, reports case after case of patients, including doctors, even heart specialists, who religiously avoided cholesterol foods and fat intake, but suffered a heart attack in spite of these measures. Passwater observes: 'Even though doctors have been warning us for fifty years that cholesterol ... is the cause of atherosclerosis (deposits in the arteries) heart disease is striking increasingly larger portions of our population and at progressively earlier ages. ... *If cholesterol reduction were effective, results would have been apparent long ago* (emphasis added).

Dr Passwater, a biochemist, admits that arteriosclerosis and atherosclerosis can be caused by cholesterol, fat, and certain calcium deposits, but, citing his proof, claims that reducing cholesterol intake not only does *not* reduce the deposits, but also does not reduce the cholesterol blood level or the onset of heart attacks. In fact, in his book he states that low cholesterol can *increase* the incidence of heart disease. He points out that research shows that earlier generations that ate gravies, fat meats, whole grains, and vegetables did not experience coronary thrombosis, so prevalent today.

Dr Passwater points out that whole milk (not skim milk) and eggs are two of our best foods. He cites one study of 804, 409 persons in which those who ate practically no eggs had more deaths from heart attacks and strokes than those who ate all the eggs they wanted.

Big Business Propaganda?

What are the reasons behind these 'scare tactics' against cholesterol and saturated fats? Brace yourself for an honest answer, as quoted in Dr Passwater's book, from Dr Teh C. Huang, a heart researcher: 'Propaganda against cholesterol and saturated fat has been going on and been well accepted, while for centuries millions of human lives have been saved by milk and eggs. Don't cut out cholesterol and saturated fats from your diet. Warnings that they lead to heart disease are scare tactics by big business.' ('Scare tactics' refers to high-profit sales of low cholesterol foods, including margarine.)

The highly nutritious natural foods, properly raised, contain natural vitamins and minerals. These foods are quite different from the highly processed foods that are so common today and from which vitamins and minerals have been removed. If any are returned to the food, they are fewer in number than those bestowed by nature, and they are usually synthetic, not natural. In addition, thousands of chemicals, colourings, fillers, and preservatives are added to foods to make them appear or taste more 'natural'.

Even fresh garden produce or fruit may be less than

WHAT TO DO ABOUT DEGENERATIVE DISEASES

nutritious, since much of this fresh food is polluted by pesticide sprays or contaminated by the highly chemicalized soil in which the food is grown, considered necessary by growers to stimulate faster growth and bigger crops. The few farmers and gardeners who grow their crops organically, which means that only natural fertilizers are used and nature controls the speed of growth, yielding a nutritious product instead of a hollow one, can't keep their produce long enough to supply all of their enthusiastic customers. Yet it is shocking that at this writing certain bureaucratic groups are attempting to ban the words 'organic' and 'natural' from labels even if the foods *are* organic and natural and therefore obviously more nutritious. Why? Because the big food processors apparently do not want such competition to the unnatural food they manufacture. You can usually tell the difference, because natural foods taste better. But the manufacturers are becoming more cunning with their masquerade and want us to believe their products are superior to natural ones.

Foods that are naturally endowed with vitamins and minerals are not only preferable; there is much information that certain vitamins and minerals may protect against heart attacks. This includes most minerals, as well as vitamins E, C, B6, and the entire B complex family.

People who are afraid to eat *any* fat and adopt a completely fat-free diet, either to avoid artery trouble or for reducing purposes, can be piling up other troubles for themselves. Our bodies need fat for various reasons. For example, a gall bladder denied fat can produce gallstones.[1] Also, without fat in the diet, the fat-soluble vitamins A, E, D, and K cannot be properly assimilated. Do not dismiss this problem lightly. Without sufficient vitamin A your vision and skin can suffer; without vitamin D, calcium, needed for bones, is not properly assimilated. Without E the heart muscle can suffer, and without K blood clotting cannot occur, leading to haemorrhages.[2] So dietary fats are crucially necessary.

Even those who avoid fat for fear of overweight may be surprised to learn that it may be easier to reduce if some fat is eaten. Adelle Davis tells the story of the model who could not lose weight until she added a few tablespoonsful of vegetable oil to her daily diet.

How to Dissolve Artery Fat and Cholesterol

There is a way to emulsify or dissolve excess fat and cholesterol deposits that may already have formed in your arteries. It can also help prevent them. This method was demonstrated by a physician.

Lester M. Morrison, who learned that the substance lecithin (pronounced lessithin) is similar to a detergent taken orally and can dissolve or emulsify artery-plugging fats and cholesterol, even excess cholesterol in the blood reported some dramatic results with his patients. They became able to walk again without difficulty if this had been a problem. They became more alert, vital, younger looking and acting in many cases. Even the yellowish plaques that had developed around their eyes were dissolved and disappeared. Dr Morrison recommended four tablespoonsful of lecithin granules daily for his patients, to be taken in juices, on cereals, salads, or however convenient. Lecithin granules, made from soyabeans, are somewhat nutty in texture but tasteless. Dr Morrison, who was interested in nutrition, also advocated at least two tablespoonsful of soya or safflower oil daily to 'provide the essential fatty acids necessary for proper nutrition.' He recommended vitamins as well, especially B, C, and E. Meanwhile, though Dr Morrison was ahead of his time with his discoveries about lecithin (additional exciting information will be discussed later), a newer type of lecithin has come on the market: liquid lecithin. Less of it is evidently necessary. One researcher found that one teaspoonful taken morning and evening could keep it in the bloodstream at all times. It has been found to be effective in reversing some other difficult diseases too, including myasthenia gravis.[3]

Dr William Donald Kelley recommends liquid lecithin, as did the late nutrition expert Dr Royal Lee. Dr Kelley recommends about one tablespoonful of it daily and believes it is better than granular or powdered lecithin (another newcomer), because it contains, he says, a new unnamed vitamin missing in the other forms. Liquid lecithin is easier for some people to take, harder for others. It looks like honey, has the consistency of honey, but there the similarity ends. It tastes like nothing and sticks to a spoon as well as to the roof of your mouth.

Preventive Artery Control

There are two schools of thought on natural or preventive artery control. One school believes in sharply restricting fats and cholesterol foods, combined with exercise. This school of thought is represented by the Longevity Research Institute, discussed previously. A second school does not worry about fats and cholesterol foods but does emphasize vitamin/mineral supplements plus lecithin to prevent the possible nutritional deficiencies that may have caused the problem in the first place. This school of thought also embraces exercise. Reporters are not supposed to have opinions, but having been a nutrition reporter for many years, I must admit that, to me, the latter method makes sense and is the easier to follow. Dr Morrison seems to stand squarely between the two groups. At the time he wrote his book he was espousing a low-fat diet, but he also used lecithin along with vitamins and minerals. He, too, by this method reversed atherosclerosis, painful angina, and other circulatory ailments.

Since you have already seen what the Longevity Institute has accomplished with its method (the low-fat diet plus exercise), let me give you two examples of recovery reported by Richard A. Passwater, an advocate of the second school of thought.

Jacobus Rinse, Ph.D., at the age of fifty-one, was found to have atherosclerosis as well as painful angina, complicated by heart spasms. He did not smoke, was not overweight, had no unusual tensions, and took sufficient exercise. He had no family history of this disease. Completely baffled, he decided he must have some nutritional deficiency, and after reading the literature avidly, decided to add one tablespoonful of lecithin granules to his breakfast cereal.

He noticed good results within a few days. The heart spasms ceased, and by the end of three months all signs of angina, even after exercising, had stopped. A year later he could again resume outdoor work and running. Even though he still could not believe it, there was no recurrence of angina up to sixteen years later, at which time he made the report.

In one group, heart attacks in one and a blood clot in another also responded to lecithin therapy. In the second case, a strict diet without eggs or butter was first used, with no improvement. Still another man, at seventy-two, who had suffered several heart attacks as well as angina, stated that he cured himself with the lecithin therapy *in three months*.

In the above cases the lecithin was included in a breakfast mixture, originated by Dr Rinse, containing brewers yeast, wheat germ, bone meal, one tablespoonful of vegetable oil, as well as the tablespoonful of lecithin granules (doubled in severe cases of atherosclerosis). These ingredients could also be taken in other ways, such as in a protein drink. In addition to the foods mentioned, supplements including 500mg. of vitamin C, 100 I.U. vitamin E and one multiple vitamin/mineral tablet were also included by the doctor for his own programme. His breakfast mixture is now available at health stores, or you can make your own.

As for the calcium deposits that the fat-cholesterol plaques seem to attract to the arteries or that may pile up in the joints of arthritis, the late Dr Jarvis, author of *Folk Medicine*[4] fame may have provided a solution. He learned that because calcium needs acid to dissolve and remain in solution instead of forming hard deposits in unwanted places, apple cider vinegar could accomplish this feat. He demonstrated it in autopsies performed after death on aged cows. Those whose rations had been 'spiked' with apple cider vinegar showed reversal of joint stiffness. For human beings Dr Jarvis recommended apple cider vinegar added to drinking water to suit their own taste and sipped throughout the day or at meals like wine. It is a refreshing drink, and many people report feeling better after adopting this practice. Some people add a bit of honey for taste.

There are other degenerative diseases, resulting from other causes. Arthritis may be caused by an inadequate diet, as well as by too little acid. But it can also be produced by stress, a cause of many ailments. Stress creates tension, jams body works, slows down circulation, and prevents nutrients from reaching various parts of the body. All manner of degenerative ailments have been traced to stress. You will find a solution for this problem in the chapter on breathing.

One example of a stress-caused instance of arthritis was the man whose wife ran away with another man; her husband became a wheelchair invalid the next day. Meanwhile, if a

WHAT TO DO ABOUT DEGENERATIVE DISEASES

heart attack or stroke should occur, it is no longer a do-it-yourself project. Call a doctor immediately!

There are other degenerative diseases which, due to lack of space, I cannot cover here, particularly since I have already written an entire book about them, including, among many others, such problems as high blood pressure and allergies. This book, *A Handbook of Natural Remedies for Common Ailments*, is available through your book or health store. However, the following pages will show you how to build health and resist illness in general.

REFERENCES
(See *Bibliography* for fuller details)

1. Linda Clark, *Stay Young Longer*.
2. ———, *Know Your Nutrition*.
3. ———, *Secrets of Health and Beauty*.
4. Jarvis, D.C., *Folk Medicine*.

7

Enzymes for Health and Youth

Enzymes are catalysts that exist in every cell of your body. They speed up or direct the activity of various body processes. They consist of proteins and are highly specific in their functions. Enzymes act as housecleaners, and because of their many functions in helping to maintain health, they are also called metabolic enzymes. We have much more to learn about these fabulous enzymes; the exact mechanism by which they act is not fully understood.

One category of enzymes that *has* been studied is the digestive enzymes, which help you digest your food. There is one type to digest fat, others to digest protein, and still others for carbohydrate and cellulose digestion. If you do not manufacture enough of your own digestive enzymes, you can buy them at a health store to help boost your own dwindling supply.

A nutritional doctor told me recently: 'I would not be alive today if it were not for the digestive enzymes I take.' The explanation is clear. You could have the best diet in the world, but if you do not digest or assimilate it, it cannot deliver the nutrition you need.

There are some specific enzymes missing in some people for the digestion of certain foods. For example, many people throughout the world lack the enzyme that digests cow's milk. Cow's milk contains a form of milk sugar known as lact*ose*. The enzyme needed to digest lactose is lact*ase*. (Many enzymes have the *ase* ending.) Babies can suffer from this enzyme lack as well as adults. A health store owner recently told me: 'I cannot drink cow's milk. I swell up with gas that lasts all day.'

Milk Enzymes

This person is not alone in such a reaction to cow's milk or anything made with it – yogurt, cheese of all kinds, etc. Many people know they are allergic to 'something', not dreaming it is milk, which they may love. It is a common problem throughout the world. I am sympathetic, since I too am a milk intolerant. Whereas a few can tolerate soured milks such as yogurt or kefir, I cannot enjoy even these. This reaction to milk is not called an allergy but an *intolerance*.

Fortunately, a solution to this serious problem has appeared as milk digestants have now been formulated. It contains lactase, the enzyme lacking in milk tolerants. The product is in tablet form and is taken orally prior to any meal containing cow's milk. For those who have tried it (and I am one) it works like a charm. But it must be taken *before*, not *during* or *after*, a meal. This product, because the ingredients previously have been scarce, has been hard to find. Health stores are now stocking it as fast as possible, as it is becoming more readily available. I have been receiving letters from many who are delighted they can now drink milk again, thanks to this excellent enzyme product.

Because milk is used in cooking and in such foods as soups, sauces, and many others, I always carry my milk digestant tablets with me when I eat away from home, even at a friend's house, and take two for insurance before a meal. Beware of substitutes.

Some people who cannot tolerate cow's milk can use goat's milk. Others cannot. Fortunately, I can. I use goat's milk that I buy directly from a goat owner. Stores are not allowed to sell goat's milk in many states because of an ordinance requiring all milk to be pasteurized. If the animals are clean, tested regularly, and the milk, milkers, and containers are hygienically clean, bacteria count has been found to be lower in raw than in pasteurized milk. Also, raw milk contains enzymes. Pasteurized milk does not.

Raw Food Enzymes

Raw foods contain enzymes that can bolster your own metabolic enzymes. But these biological enzymes are destroyed at a temperature of 119°F (48°C), or to be on the safe side, above normal body temperature, that is, above 98.4°F (36.9°C). For example, if you cook a raw green tomato, the enzymes that could have turned it red are destroyed. So the more raw food you eat the better.

One doctor has claimed that if you are beginning to feel your age, it is because the enzymes in your body are becoming fewer and weaker. This results in a withering process, which is observable in people and animals. In fact, tests conducted on older people revealed that inadequate eating of enzymes in raw foods may lead to wrinkling of the skin, thinning of the hair, sagging of muscles and figure, as well as lack-lustre eyes.[1]

This does not mean that all foods need to be eaten raw. Some foods should be cooked, especially meat, which may contain parasites (such as trichina in pork). Also, some people, as they add years, are often unable to masticate their food properly. There are two solutions here. If you have no chewing problems, eat as many vegetables as possible raw, or undercook them as in the Oriental method of stir-fry, which leaves vegetables bright coloured and crunchy, not pale and limp. If you do have chewing problems, get a juicer and juice your raw fruits and vegetables, which leaves the enzymes intact, or put them in a blender to make into soups. Freezing does not kill enzymes, merely inactivates them temporarily, but it does rob foods of some vitamins and minerals, due to the hot-water blanching process used prior to freezing. And the longer the frozen foods remain in the freezer, the greater the loss of nutrients.

But all foods need not be eaten raw. Some are even better eaten in cooked form. Carrots, for example, have been found to release more carotene (a form of vitamin A) than raw carrots. But if you do cook vegetables, don't drown them in water and then pour the liquid down the sink! Water leaches out vitamins and minerals, so cook them quickly in a minimum of water and save the liquid for soups or to add to vegetable juices. Another and very easy method is to steam vegetables. You will find a small, folding stainless steel steamer basket in hardware and department stores, which you can use in an ordinary pan with the water just up to the bottom of the steamer. Most vegetables take only minutes to be done, and there's no mess to clean up.

However, raw food enzymes are so important to health and appearance that some nutritionists advise eating at least 50 per cent of your food raw.

Other Important Digestants

In addition to digestive enzymes, there is another important digestant, hydrochloric acid (abbreviated as HCL), which you can buy at health stores. It digests protein, calcium, and iron. Doctors formerly believed that HCL manufactured in the body begins to dwindle only as one ages. This is no longer necessarily true. Due to stress, lack of B vitamins, and other unknown factors, many people of all ages are becoming afflicted with this deficiency. Even some babies who do not thrive after birth have picked up and improved when given a tiny amount of HCL in their formula.

Although I have thoroughly covered the subject elsewhere,[2] I will repeat the highlights here. Many people, influenced by television commercials trying to sell antacids, believe they have 'acid stomach'. Not only is this usually untrue, but even doctors who do not understand the widespread deficiency of this digestant may erroneously prescribe an antacid when they should prescribe HCL. The reason: *The symptoms of too much acid are identical with those of too little acid.* Although there are a few tests for HCL deficiency, including the unpleasant one of stomach pumping, you can find out for yourself if you need it.

Dr Hugh Tuckey, now retired, is one of the few doctors who has thoroughly studied HCL and has done years of research on the subject. After trying many different compounds of HCL, he has found that *Hydrochloric Acid, Betaine, with Pepsin* (available at health stores) is the most effective and easiest to take.

To determine whether you need it, or if so, how much, Dr Tuckey suggests taking one tablet after your main protein meal. If you experience any uncomfortable symptoms, such as burning, he suggests drinking a full glass of water immediately to wash it away. At the next protein meal, try only a half tablet, he says. Gradually you learn how much suits your needs and at which meal to take it.

People vary in the need for HCL, even on a daily basis. Extreme fatigue or stress at mealtime stops its manufacture, so watch it! Think or discuss only pleasant subjects while eating. Incidentally, I know several people who manufacture no HCL at all. Two of them were born with this deficiency; the other acquired a partial loss along the way. I have received letters from numerous readers who told me that their gas and other digestive problems disappeared upon taking HCL. So not only does the need vary in different people, but many people who should be taking protein and are not doing so believe that protein does not agree with them. They are so right! They lack this compound needed to digest the protein.

The digestive enzyme that helps the body to handle starch, or carbohydrates, is called *amylase*. Still more important is a digestive enzyme that digests fat! This is called *lipase*, and could it be an overlooked factor in those with artery clogging? It is possible that the fats, instead of being digested, are being deposited in the arteries instead of dissolved and mobilized out of the body. Lipase and other digestive enzymes described below are available at health stores. Read the labels on digestive enzyme containers to be sure they contain what you need.

Other enzymes include *trypsin* and *chymotrypsin*, derived from the pancreas, which help pancreas digestion. Some people who suffer from pancreatitis apparently cannot digest carbohydrates; others cannot digest fats. My own mother was one of the latter types. When her doctor discovered that she had a defective pancreas, he restricted her diet to a pitiful number of foods for the rest of her life. I supplied her with the whole pancreatin product (from a health store), which contains all the pancreatic enzymes, and she ate whatever she wanted from that time on for twenty-five years before she died of other causes.

You will have to learn to analyze what enzymes you may need. More people may have a fat intolerance than may be realized. Gas can result from fat intolerance, as well as from protein indigestion or from intolerance to cow's milk.

Although the former method of preventing fat intolerance was to put people on a strict fat-free diet, the newer approach is to use perhaps a medium amount of fat to lighten the burden on the body and supply fat-digesting enzymes and vitamins. These include not only lipase, but vitamin B_6, and, in some cases, *occasional* bile salts. Lecithin is also a tremendous help.

Health stores stock various kinds of digestive enzymes, some separately, others in combination, since it has been noted that if one digestive enzyme is at low ebb, others may be too.

Watch your carbohydrates! Man-made concoctions like pies, cakes, cookies, candies, sugary desserts, as well as alcohol, and too many cooked foods create a great drain on the digestive enzyme system. Natural foods, such as raw fruits and vegetables, contain their own enzymes. Fresh fruits are a better choice for those with a 'sweet tooth' than man-made 'dead food sweets'. But do not overdo even fresh fruits. Nutritionists are learning that, because of their sugar content, even though natural, no more than two fruits eaten daily is preferable to going on an unlimited raw fruit binge.

Summary

To summarize why enzymes are so important, here are some statements from two researchers on the subject. Few chemists or biochemists really understand the full function of enzymes, so the following information from those who are experts on the subject is indeed valuable.

Dr Justa Smith, a noted biochemist and former Director of Research, Department of Nutrition, Rosary Hill College, Buffalo, New York, says: 'Body cells are largely controlled by enzymes.'

Dr Edward Howell, a scientist who has spent forty years in studying enzymes, feels that enzymes may spell the difference between health and disease, even life or death. He also feels that too few enzymes cause premature ageing. Since cooking at a temperature of 119°F (48°C), he says, destroys enzymes, the body, although it contains many enzymes for many different purposes, becomes eventually depleted because of eating so much cooked food. It puts a great burden on the body enzyme system, including defence against disease. Dr Howell believes that by adding digestive enzymes to our meals to balance the cooked food we eat, and by adding raw food wherever possible, we relieve the body's burden of a limited enzyme potential. Since some people cannot tolerate a 100 per cent raw diet, Dr Howell's solution is to compensate for the cooked food you do eat with enzymes from as much raw food as you can eat, plus digestive enzyme supplements (from health shops). If you dry your own foods, he cautions you to use a temperature no higher than 110°F (43°C). He also favours freeze drying. Dr Howell believes that digestive enzymes should be taken *with* your meals, not at the end of the meal. Otherwise your body may have already started to deplete its own enzyme supply. He also believes that enzymes are a missing link in health and well-being, as well as a factor in premature ageing.

Do not ask your health food operator to tell you what digestive enzyme product to use. Outside pressures levelled against health stores can claim they are 'prescribing medicine without a licence', and the operator could land in gaol. (It has happened.) Ask to see all of the digestive enzymes in stock, read the labels, and decide for yourself. You may have to try several before eventually finding the one that suits you best.

REFERENCES
(See *Bibliography* for fuller details)

1. Linda Clark, *Stay Young Longer*.
2. ——, *Secrets of Health and Beauty*.

8

Other Foods for Rejuvenation

Dr José Froimovich of Chile has proved that the correct nutrients can help rehabilitate the ageing. Dr Froimovich is not a newcomer to this field. He has been a specialist in gerontology for over thirty-five years. He has been nominated for the Nobel Prize in Medicine for his successful work in reversing or postponing ageing by a formula he developed known as FGF-60. It also maintains the body tissue, he says, of people in all age brackets.

Dr Froimovich explains: 'All studies show that people should live between 100 and 120 years. The fact that most people don't is that at one time or another their systems are deprived of certain substances.'

Dr Froimovich's formula, FGF-60, is a combination of sixty vitamins, minerals, hormones, and extracts of organs, all of which he considers necessary to retard ageing. He says: 'We can reverse many of the symptoms of ageing, although we do not claim this to be rejuvenation. By using FGF-60 a person can see a little better, hear a little better, have a better love life, have more strength.'

The formula can apparently prevent such diseases associated with old age as stroke and heart attack. Wrinkles become smoother, hair stops falling, energy increases. People who begin the use of this formula can in many cases soon play strenuous sports with safety.

Dr Froimovich has performed over 15,000 tests with a hundred men and fifty women. The patients were approximately seventy-five years old and were subjected to nearly every known medical test before and after the administration of the formula.

A film has been made showing the progress of the patients on FGF-60, which was supplied in capsules, some for men, others for women (presumably differing only in male and female sex hormones). The film shows the elderly patients entering Dr Froimovich's clinic on canes, crutches, in wheelchairs, and on stretchers. Thirty days after treatment the same patients are shown taking exercises such as walking, running, jogging, even playing basketball. One before-and-after photograph shows a seventy-six-year-old man before taking the formula. He looks closer to ninety. In the picture, taken three years later when he was seventy-nine, he looks closer to forty.

Now I am sure you are all agog as to where you can purchase this formula. You can't, at least, not for the time being. I do not know the exact ingredients of Dr Froimovich's formula, nor would I presume even to guess at the work of such a distinguished scientist. But as a nutrition researcher for many years I can suggest many of the probable essentials the body needs for repair, based on years of study by other scientists. I am sure that Dr Froimovich would not hold it against us if we were to try to help ourselves with what nutritional information is now available. In fact, if we don't take advantage of such knowledge, some people may not be here when the formula is released!

Nutritional scientists have already isolated more than sixty nutrients the body needs for health, cell, and gland building. These nutrients include all known vitamins, minerals, hormones, glandular substances, as well as certain fats and special foods.

Since we do not yet have access to the Froimovich formula, and since there is no monopoly on nutritional knowledge already available, in self-defence we will have to look elsewhere for similar help. At this point I called in several nutritional consultants to help set up a programme to bring similar results in the reversal of ageing. You can begin to use this new programme *now* without further delay. Who knows? This programme may contain even more helpful information not found elsewhere, perhaps even in the Froimovich programme. You will find it in this book, beginning with the next chapter.

REFERENCES
(See *Bibliography* for fuller details)

1. Linda Clark, *Know Your Nutrition*.

9

Beginning Your Rejuvenation Programme

The information in the following chapters is your passport to rejuvenation, providing it is used properly by adjusting it to your own individual needs.

We are all different. Roger J. Williams, Ph.D., a famous biochemist of the University of Texas, has written many books on this subject. He points out that each of us is as different as our fingerprints, our blood types, and in many other unsuspected ways, yet we can still be considered 'normal'. He calls attention to the fact that hearts, livers, and other organs pictured in medical textbooks vary in shape and size from person to person. No two are exactly alike.

Another example of individual difference: A recent newspaper article reported that one woman was found to have a heart on her *right* side, even though everyone knows it should be on the *left* side! Yet this woman is considered to be in 'normal' health.

Textbook pictures of stomachs also vary. Is it any wonder then that digestion and assimilation may vary from person to person? Recent research proves that they do.

One of the first steps to take in your rejuvenation programme is to start giving your body proper fuel to help wake up your glands, improve your cells, and increase your energy. There are certain foods that can act as tools to accomplish these goals. Some substances are basic needs for everyone. Others must be chosen for your own individual needs. For example, we all need water to drink. We all need food, and since so much food these days is refined or filled with additives and chemicals for colouring, preservation, and other reasons, vitamins and minerals have been pushed out to make room for the additives. So usually we also need vitamin and mineral supplements to replace those that have been removed from our food. The question is, what supplements do you need? How many? How strong (meaning what potency) should they be? This is where individual differences come into the picture. Vitamin A is a good example.

Our Varying Needs

Some people need and can safely take huge amounts of vitamin A. Yet I, for one, cannot take any at all. So I have to choose *foods* that contain vitamin A in order to get my allotment. After all, to get well and stay well we really need *all* vitamins and minerals (which appear together in natural foods), not just one vitamin here and another mineral there. For best results we usually *need the whole works*! But since we are all different, one person, even members of the same family, may need more or less than others.

I cannot tell you exactly what you need or how much, because I do not know. To be absolutely truthful, neither does anyone else. The newer doctors are learning this fact, and they will suggest that you try certain supplements and see how you react to them. They believe that you know your own body better than anyone else, and since they cannot follow you around and watch your reactions from minute to minute, hour to hour, it is *your* job to find out what you need as well as how much or how little. We can all supply clues. For example, you will find each vitamin, mineral, and food described in my book *Know Your Nutrition*, showing what these supplements are supposed to do, have done for others, and *may* do for you. I cannot repeat the entire book in this one, so I suggest you look for it in paperback or hardcover at health stores to use as a reference.

Since you now realize that your glands and organs may differ from those of others, it will come as no surprise that you may not thrive on the diet that keeps your husband or wife or best friend in good health.

There are hundreds of variables between people. One person may be of a more lethargic, sluggish temperament and have a slower digestion-assimilation system. Often this type needs less food and does not get hungry for hours after eating. On the other hand, some people burn up energy rapidly, even in sedentary occupations, and a short while after eating they become ravenous again. These people may need more food, or may need to eat smaller meals more often, since their digestion may not be able to accommodate large meals at one time.

Researchers, including Drs Roger J. Williams, Paul Eck, George Watson, the late Mary M.B. Allen, Arthur Robinson, who is a chemist and director of the Linus Pauling Institute (all Ph.D.s; as well as Dr Edward Howell and William Donald Kelley, DDS, nutrition researcher, are turning up some surprising findings. It appears that not all people should be vegetarians, but some will feel better, stronger, and avoid anaemia if they eat meat, preferably beef, at least about five times a week. Since, according to these researchers, there are people who cannot assimilate some of the individual amino acids (protein factors), this meat diet would actually make *them* ill. There are others whom vegetarianism can eventually make ill! (You will find such an example farther on in this chapter.) Some people can apparently get all the nourishment they need from vegetables, fruits, seeds, and nuts. Others, even vegetarians, feel more energetic on a lacto-ovo vegetarian diet, meaning they include dairy products and eggs in their diet. So it is never safe to generalize.

Professionals suggest that you alone can determine your own digestive-assimilation type, known to the scientists as metabolism, and there are many variations or subheads within well-defined metabolism categories. For instance, disliked foods, allergies, or food intolerances can interfere with the digestion-assimilation of some foods for some people. Even the area in which you live may be a factor (due to air pollution, noise, and other conditions beyond your control), as well as climate (too much heat or humidity, which may take away your appetite). It is generally known that emotions can affect your metabolism. If you live or work for someone you loathe, you are going to become tense, which can, in turn, affect your digestion and assimilation. The best way to find out your own hang-ups is to outline a type of diet for a month that allows for your own idiosyncracies, follow it faithfully, then evaluate it before continuing further. You may have found that your body chemistry has changed or that you can or cannot eat certain foods you used originally.

Allow time, also, to make a decision on vegetarianism. Almost everyone feels better, at first, on a vegetarian diet, since it is also a cleansing diet. But for some people, if prolonged, anaemia, weakness, fatigue, and nerve involvement may develop, which can be serious if not caught in time.

Remember that *no two people are alike*.

It is not fair to your mate or your children to force your diet on them, or to expect their diet to agree with yours. Each person needs to take time out for a trial-and-error period to discover what is best for him or her.

Listening to Your Body

There is one warning in connection with choosing the foods you think you need. Some people brag that their bodies tell them what they need. There is truth in the supposition that we should listen to our body language, but this body language really means that we should notice what happens after we eat certain foods, not necessarily follow overpowering cravings blindly.

There is a 'wisdom of the body', but there are also false cravings. These include coffee, excessive use of salt, sweets, alcohol, and tobacco. They are unnatural cravings and should NOT be heeded. They are all habit forming and can throw off your entire body chemistry if you give in to them on an unlimited or a regular basis.

On the plus side, for example, some people crave sour foods. This may well be a clue to a lack of digestive acid (HCL), which you really may need. Even those wild cravings of pregnant women may be important body language, and should be treated with respect. I knew a pregnant woman who woke up one winter night and had a violent craving for seafood. This might be translated into a need for minerals (richly present in seafood). So listen to what your body is trying to tell you, but pay no attention to the continuous coffee, sugar, alcohol, or tobacco route. Taking a bit of protein (nuts, cheese, or whatever you like) may satisfy your craving, which leads us right back to a nutrient that has long been considered a *must* for glands, as well as for anti-ageing.

Protein Deficiency

There is much speculation that those who are getting along in years may be suffering from a protein deficiency, and those who also lack energy may be short in protein. This makes a great deal of sense, since glands, which keep your body running efficiently, are made of protein. Even if your metabolic type seems to indicate that you are a nonmeat-eating candidate, it is still true that you may need protein in some other form. If you are averse to meat, perhaps you can at least eat dairy products. Health Stores abound in protein powders and brewer's yeast, one of our finest foods, is a powerful protein substance, yet contains no animal protein.

It is possible that you may believe you cannot eat protein because it does not seem to agree with you. This is perhaps because you lack hydrochloric acid, which digests protein (as well as calcium and iron). This you can add as a dietary supplement, as explained previously. So if you choose the right type of protein for your metabolism and add the digestive enzymes to help assimilate the protein, you may find your energy returning by leaps and bounds. One of my daughters, the minute she feels fatigued or slightly weak, rushes to the kitchen, stirs up a tablespoonful of brewer's yeast powder or flakes in water, tomato juice, or hot consommé (the canned variety is delicious), and her energy is restored within a few minutes and lasts for hours, quite different from the effects of a cup of coffee, or some sugar, which provides energy for a few minutes, then leaves you feeling worse than before, leading to a yo-yo syndrome of wanting more and more.

One woman told me recently that her boss, whom she converted away from being a 'coffeeholic' by giving him brewer's yeast at coffee-break time, will suddenly look a bit wobbly and say to her, 'I know what's wrong with me. Will you please fix me some brewer's yeast?'

The weakness, common to people who are always looking for something to shore up their energy, is actually a condition called hypoglycaemia, or low blood sugar. Tobacco, sweets, or alcohol do not give lasting help. Protein does. But protein can do much more:

The word 'protein', coined by a Dutch chemist in 1839,

means 'of first importance'. After water, fat, and bones are removed, what is left in the human body represents 95 per cent protein. But we use up protein rapidly in our daily activities and energy expenditure. Even stress can use up protein. This protein needs to be replaced on a regular basis; some nutritionists believe daily, others believe with each meal.

The Importance of Protein

Meanwhile, we cannot ignore facts. Those who are getting older, please pay particular attention to the following facts:

— Our muscles, which include our heart, liver, kidneys, even our eyes, are basically protein. Lack of protein can leave them weak and flabby.
— The liver, perhaps the most important organ in our bodies after the heart, needs adequate protein to function properly.
— A hormone, a chemical regulator, is a protein.
— The genes, which influence heredity, are proteins.
— The secretion of the thyroid gland is a protein.
— Insulin, manufactured by the pancreas, is a protein.
— Secretion of the pituitary gland, a master gland, is a protein.
— Antibodies, which defend us against infection, are proteins.
— Enzymes, which control digestion and a host of other functions, are proteins.
— Haemoglobin, the red colouring substance in the blood, is a protein.
— The body must have protein to repair a wound, a cut, or any other injury.

Even your appearance and good looks depend upon protein. Without enough protein the muscles in your face begin to droop, skin begins to wrinkle. Researchers have stated that the withering of old age may actually be due to lack of protein.

Adelle Davis puts it more succinctly: 'Since your body structure is largely protein, a deficiency can bring about age with depressing speed ... Muscles lose tone, wrinkles appear, ageing creeps in, and you, my dear, are going to pot'[2] (and she does not mean the kind you smoke).

Many people who are getting older complain of not feeling well. Lack of protein can play a part here too.

BEGINNING YOUR REJUVENATION PROGRAMME 51

Protein deficiency has been found to cause the following:
   Anaemia
   Kidney disease
   Peptic ulcer
   Poor wound healing
   Lack of resistance to infection
   Irritability
   Fatigue
   Low blood pressure
   Wasting, weak, and flabby muscles
   Poor circulation
   Mental retardation in children
   Oedema (water storage)
   Poor vision

Since we have examined different metabolism categories, we now know that some people can be vegetarians, others should not be. (I have covered the subject of vegetarianism in depth in another book.[3])

Meat, fish, eggs, and other dairy products contain all of the essential amino acids (protein factors). If one amino acid is missing, the rest are useless to your body. So complete protein is important, which explains why meat, fish, fowl, and dairy products are found to have the highest biological value, and therefore are classed as complete proteins. Nuts, vegetables, and fruits do not usually contain either enough protein or all of the eight essential amino acids your body needs simultaneously.

Let me give you just one example here. Mary Jane Hungerford, a respected nutritionist, tells the story of a nineteen-year-old boy who belonged to a religious sect that required its members to be vegetarians. He was required, also, to eat only raw food. As a result he had a complete nervous breakdown, followed by a second one; developed a serious skin rash; was skin-and-bones, as well as mentally confused. He lived largely on fruits and believed (mistakenly) that protein disagreed with him.

Your glands need protein to keep you from falling apart. They also need vitamins and minerals for best performance. But one of the best things to feed glands is glands! There is proof. Radioactive tracers have found that when you feed liver to the body, it heads for the liver to give it a lift. Brain goes to brain, pancreas goes to pancreas, or, more surprising, if you mix all these glandular substances together, the body sorts them out and delivers them to the right places. How about that for efficiency?

So pamper your glands so that they will pamper you and help keep you feeling and looking younger. There are glandular substances now available in tablet form, and I will tell you about them in the next chapter.

REFERENCES
(See *Bibliography* for fuller details)

1. Linda Clark, *Secrets of Health and Beauty*.
2. Adelle Davis, *Let's Eat Right to Keep Fit*.
3. Linda Clark, *The Best of Linda Clark* (an anthology). See chapter 'Vegetarians Beware'.

10

Rejuvenation Therapy

We have already emphasized the importance of glands. But why are they so important in ageing?

Although in a few cases during ageing some glands can become overactive, usually at this time of life the vital processes of the body tend to slow down, particularly glandular functions, enzyme production, and cell rebuilding. Assimilation may also become inefficient, resulting in retention of waste products, toxins, and body poisons. This, in turn, can lead to joint stiffness, weakened muscles, demineralization of the skeletal structure, a loss of balance and a host of other disturbances. Some people develop outright degenerative diseases. (These ailments can, of course, appear at any age.) Many investigators believe that the basic cause of such disturbances may be due to toxins or deficiency of repair material in the body.

Replacing the Body Repair Materials

Tests show that many of these so-called 'ageing' symptoms have been reversed in various degrees by the simple use of an improved diet and the use of needed digestive enzymes, vitamins, minerals, proteins, glandular substances, and other repair materials the body originally contained but which are now dwindling. Fortunately, they can be replaced, and the body can use the replaced substances as repair materials to heal itself. The rate of recovery depends upon how deficient in cell-building nutrients a person may be, how long the condition has existed, and how serious it is, as well as the rapidity of the body uptake of these substances. The biological-nutritional concept is a simple, and almost incredible, concept (to some doctors), yet it actually works. It has happened again and again.

If these concentrated substances – which are foods, not medicine – are taken *regularly*, the body can also use them not only to repair itself but to prevent future illness and maintain health. It is already known that living cells have been kept alive for indefinite periods by the use of such nutrients. (Dr Alexis Carrel's experiment with the heart, discussed in Chapter 3, is an example).

Raw nutrients are often more effective for body conversion into repair materials than those subjected to great heat through cooking. Glandular substances derived from raw organ meats have been known for years for their therapeutic effects. The American Indians, after killing a buffalo, always sought and consumed the raw liver first. Even though fire was available for cooking, they had learned that raw liver was more effective than cooked. Today much of our food is overcooked, overprocessed (removing many nutrients sensitive to heat), and some nutritionists believe this is one reason for the increasing rate of physical – and even mental – afflictions.

Gland Therapy

It is for this reason that the rejuvenation programme presented here is based upon 'raw' glandular concentrates, meaning they have been processed at only 37°C (98.6°F) and still retain enzymes and other heat-sensitive nutrients. You have read, earlier in this book, that radioactive tracers show how a glandular substance, when given to the body, can make a bee-line to the identical gland or glands in the body to begin its repair work.

But where can you find this gland therapy?

There are several methods of gland therapy and for information about these and for supplies of the glandular extracts write to Bio-Nutritional Products, PO Box 389, Harrison, NY 10528, U.S.A.

If you cannot find a doctor to help you with his expertise, do not lose hope. You might prefer to consider a spa. Let's look at those that provide what is called fresh cell therapy by injection. This method of treatment was introduced by the late Dr Paul Niehans, of Switzerland, and is now available to the public in a number of European clinics. Patients eager for quick rejuvenation went to the Niehans clinic in Vevey,

Switzerland, where fresh cells, or glands, taken from slaughtered animals were rushed, while still warm, to the waiting patients and administered by injection. It is said that among those who were 'rejuvenated' by the Niehans fresh cell therapy were personages of world-wide fame – the heads of state of various countries, as well as a renowned pope.

I have talked with people who travelled to Europe for this therapy while Dr Niehans was alive. I asked them frankly if they felt it helped them. I received the same answer from an average man who had feared getting old and from an internationally known actress who makes no secret of her perpetual search for youth. I have since talked with a large number of people who have received similar treatment at an existing spa not located in Europe. They all report almost identical results. In most cases the effect was good, perhaps even dramatic, at the outset (for several months in some cases). But these good effects did not seem to endure for long, they told me.

Since the cost of the original Niehans treatment was so high, including travel, housing, hospitalization, as well as the treatment itself, which was extremely expensive, only the independently wealthy could afford to go once, let alone return for 'recharges'.

Nutritional Gland Therapy

Nutritionists and other experts, who have studied glandular therapy from a nutritional standpoint, believe that an initial injection of fresh cells is somewhat similar to a quick recharge of your car battery on a frosty morning. It will restore your battery temporarily and get you where you want to go for the time being, but is also a reminder that a new battery may eventually be needed.

According to these experts there is a better way. If the nutrients (oral glandular substances, vitamins, minerals, proteins) are *fed on a continuous basis*, a deficiency will most likely not take place, or once the body glands have been reactivated, *the recharging will be continuous*, since they will be receiving the necessary fuel *regularly*, not on a temporary recharge basis only. Your body battery would regenerate itself.

It is no doubt true that if you can take advantage of the injection method, the sluggish glands may be initially reactivated more quickly. Or, if you have the services of a doctor who can determine through medical tests exactly what dietary glands and other supplements you need, results may also be more rapid. In any case it is up to you to provide your body with the continuous or follow-up daily fuel needed for the cells, glands, and organs to perpetuate their health. If you use the do-it-yourself method, it may take a little longer to nudge your sluggish glands into activity, but not only can it be done, it *has been done*. So if you do not have outside help, you need not feel that life has passed you by. Even if you can take advantage of the faster injection therapy at a clinic, it is advisable to follow it up with the continuous method through diet after you arrive home. It is also more convenient and less expensive.

Whole Gland Concentrates

There are now available some newer gland concentrates, which are not *extracts* of glands but the *concentrates* of the whole gland. These are made without sugar, starch, salt, and for those who may be intolerant to some foods, they also do not contain wheat, corn, soy, or yeast derivatives. These products are processed at body temperature (98.4°F/36.9°C) and are available by mail from Bio-Nutritional Products (see page 54).

In order to learn which ones you need, you should ask for a list at your health store. If you do not have a doctor knowledgeable in such matters, you use the homoeopathic approach for yourself, which is based on the principle that 'like helps like'. In other words, if you believe that you are having trouble with a certain gland, you can take the equivalent glandular concentrate for a while and see if it helps (it will not hurt you if you do not need it).

Caroline Cropp, a nutrition consultant, has reported that many people realize suddenly that they are feeling better. Because good reports are coming in from their use, as well as because of the convenience of getting them in health stores, I have built the rejuvenation programme around these glandular concentrates.

After you use the individual glandular substances you think

you may need, there is a combination product that includes ten glands for maintenance and further preventive purposes.

But before you begin your home programme and choose your glandular products, there is a preliminary step to take.

Cleansing Programme

Because waste products may have accumulated in your body over the years, before you begin your rejuvenation programme, you may first wish to give your body some internal cleansing. Waste products can clog the intestinal walls and other areas, interfering with the absorption of the new and natural repair materials you plan to feed your body later. Those who have first used a cleansing method report better and quicker results.

There are several cleansing methods from which to choose. You may already have a favourite one you have used before with success. If so, this may be the time to use it again. If you do not have your own, I will share with you the one I use. It helps me and has helped others. You may or may not find equal success with it, but at least it is safe to try.

I do not believe in fasting with water alone except under medical supervision. The reason is that though fasting has been recommended in the Bible, conditions in our times are different than in biblical days. We have accumulated and absorbed many contaminants and poisons from our polluted atmosphere, water, and food, which are then stored in our fatty tissues. DDT is one example. On a water fast alone these poisons are released too quickly into the bloodstream and can become a source of self-poisoning. Some water-alone fasters have become dangerously ill. A juice fast or raw vegetable or fresh fruit fast would be considered safer.

The method I use was originated by Stanley A. Burroughs. He calls his programme the Master Cleanser. I have found that for me it cleanses my body of stored poisons, toxins, and mucus; helps clean the kidney and digestive systems; improves the bloodstream; removes some unwanted weight that has piled up in the wrong places; and in general increases my energy and feeling of well-being. I always feel and look years younger after following it for several days (you can stop any time you wish to do so). You can even cheat occasionally (as I do) if the programme gets boring and you prefer a change in liquids. Here is the Burroughs method:

Combine the juice of ½ lemon with two tablespoonsful of a specific type of sweetening, and add to an 8 fl.oz. (225ml) glass of hot water. These sweeteners are a *must*, according to Mr Burroughs, to balance the lemon and achieve desired results. The only sweeteners allowed are any kind of unsulphured molasses: For example, Barbados or blackstrap. Some people who have trouble with these, since they are slightly laxative (though usually a good thing in a cleansing programme), use pure maple syrup with Mr Burroughs's blessing. He does not condone honey for this programme.

You are to drink this concoction, he says, from six to twelve times a day, whenever you feel hungry. Be sure to use a straw. Both lemon juice and molasses, if left on the teeth, can erode enamel. In any case, rinse your mouth with clear water after drinking, just to be sure. Take no other food during the full time of the diet.

Most people use the mixture about six times daily. If you are not eliminating properly, Mr Burroughs suggests an herb laxative tea, available at health food stores.

Mr Burroughs assures us there is no danger in this programme; the only thing you can lose, he says, is mucus, waste, and disease. He reports that healthy tissue is not affected. But he does warn not to vary the amount of lemon juice per glass.

Now what do you do after you have decided to stop this programme? Here are Mr Burroughs's suggestions. Eat, as often as you are hungry, a soup made of fresh vegetables only or steamed brown rice. On the third day he believes normal eating can be resumed. Coming off the programme correctly is crucial!

One of the benefits of this cleansing plan is that the molasses, particularly blackstrap, is rich in minerals, as well as being a natural laxative. So you are really feeding the body as you cleanse it. Any cleansing method calling for little or no solid food is uncomfortable at first, since your stomach is shrinking and putting up a fight. The first two days are the hardest. Usually, by the third day you couldn't care less, particularly since you are feeling so much better. Mr

Burroughs says you can continue this plan for ten days, but I believe each of us has to decide for himself how long to keep on with it. There is no point in letting yourself become weak, and I am inclined to think that *great* weakness is a sign to *stop*, or if you continue after that, do so only under a doctor's supervision.

The nice part of this cleansing programme is that you need not really suffer from hunger. Whenever you feel hunger pangs you can drink the mixture or cheat with something else, such as fresh juice (but no solids), although I sometimes grind up the lemon peel in the blender together with the juice and add it for bulk. The peel contains the vitamin C complex, known as bioflavonoids, so is beneficial. It also helps satisfy hunger pangs.

Some Further Cleansing Approaches

Dr John R. Christopher, a well-known herbalist, gives helpful tips for detoxifying the body. He describes an herbal mixture that cleans out the faecal impaction in the lower intestines or lower bowel. This mixture is not considered habit forming, does not cause griping, and is not a medicine but a corrective food.

Still another cleansing approach has been contributed by Caroline Cropp, nutrition consultant, which provides the glandular concentrates I mentioned earlier. It is well known that the liver is the filter for body poisons. Thus raw liver on a gland-to-gland basis has been found essential to detoxify the liver as well as the rest of the body, by easing the burden of the toxin-filtering process by the hard-working liver. 'The whole body can benefit', says Ms Cropp, 'if we keep the liver clean'. Some of these benefits, she says, are a more glowing and blemish-free complexion, relief from constipation, renewed energy and stamina. Ms Cropp reports that her own teenage son experienced a remission of acne by taking eight raw liver concentrate tablets daily for two weeks. For a pre-cleansing programme prior to the rejuvenation programme she suggests taking thirty tablets of the raw liver product daily for approximately three weeks (together with a regular diet), followed thereafter by five to ten tablets daily for preventive purposes.

Choosing Your Glandular Aids

Meanwhile, she repeats, when you begin taking your organ concentrates, you choose them by the 'like-helps-like' principle of homoeopathy. In other words, if you have a kidney problem, you choose the kidney concentrate. If you have a thyroid problem, you would choose the thyroid raw organ concentrate. And so on. After the one- to six-month period, during which time Ms Cropp finds improvement has usually taken place, you might wish to switch from the individual organ concentrates to the multiple organ product.

(Please remember that neither health store operators, nor Ms Cropp, nor I are authorized to prescribe which organ substance you need.)

Some of the possible benefits reported to Ms Cropp by doctors experienced in glandular therapy are:

Spleen and Thymus glands act to help the body's immunization against virus and infections. These glandular substances are available in the glandular concentrates.

Placenta has recently been reported by the Russians as successful for reversing or preventing ageing. Dr Niehans used placenta injections to help improve memory, promote better energy, fight fatigue, and affect almost every gland, including the sex glands. It is used extensively in cell therapy and has often turned the tide from sickness to health. Placenta is rich in RNA and DNA factors, so necessary for cell rejuvenation. Placenta is also available in organ concentrate form. Many women are concerned about using the sex hormone products, since there has been so much publicity citing them as a cause of cancer. Here is the most recent concept.

There is a difference between *hormones* (such as oestrogen) taken separately from the sexual glands, which merely stimulate, and the *whole gland* concentrate, which helps rebuild or supply the waning body gland. The concentrate of the whole ovary can be used by menopausal women who have stopped producing oestrogen. The ovary glandular substance can thus help the body ovary produce its own natural oestrogen, which in turn may help body rejuvenation. This product is called Gonadotrophic F (female), whereas orchic tissue, which has a similar rejuvenation effect on males, is called Gonadotrophic M (male). Prostate glandular concentrate has often helped regulate an enlarged prostate.

Raw heart glandular concentrate is designed to give support to the heart. Other products include the organ concentrates of stomach, digestive enzymes, lymph, mammary, adrenal, pituitary, eye, bone, pancreas, thyroid, kidney, parotid gland, brain, and uterus. In fact, a product for almost anything that is wrong with you is now available in a glandular concentrate substance.

In addition to glandular and cell substances you will need proper fuel for your body in the form of vitamins and *particularly* minerals – recent research has pin-pointed that minerals may be a common denominator in non-ageing. These nutrients are found in carefully chosen foods.

Now that you are off junk food, there is no reason to buy it or store it in your cupboard or refrigerator to tempt you in a weak moment. Stock up instead on natural foods, including fruits, raw vegetables, proteins that agree with you. Before long you should begin to feel and see the good results of your programme.

Certain foods are more powerful than others, somewhat like high octane fuel, for the continuous repair of your body, tissues, cells, organs, and glands. Let's next look at these foods and other helps.

11

Power Foods

We cannot live on supplements alone. It would take a huge tablet or capsule to include enough of these nutrient needs by the body. Many nutritionists and nutritional doctors believe it is better to get the nutrients already discovered (plus the unknowns as yet undiscovered, which do occur in nature) in *foods* if possible, and then supplement the foods with extra vitamins and minerals in tablet or capsule form as needed. There are certain special foods, often called wonder foods, that contain more of the above nutrients than ordinary foods and thus help build stronger cells and provide more energy. We will look at these power foods shortly. They are a plus value and save you money, as well as preventing you from eating too many calories.

Live Foods

Live foods, which are uncooked foods, contain more nutrients, as a rule, than cooked or processed foods. Live foods, as we have found, also contain enzymes of many kinds that cooked foods do not.

In addition to raw, or live, foods there are also life-giving foods, something quite different from just raw foods. Brown Landone once wrote about such foods – he called them 'auxin foods'[1] – which seem to carry an electrical charge or growth factor. Studies made on old, decrepit rats, the equivalent of ninety-year-old humans, showed that when given these auxins, or life-promoting, foods the aged rats were eventually transformed, and their bodies began to grow younger. One of the auxin foods is seed sprouts, like those eaten by the Chinese. Dr Howell states that *sprouts have the highest concentration of enzymes of all foods.* They are also rich in vitamins as well as auxins. They are becoming available in many food markets, but if they are not available in your area, you can make your own.

There are many good gadgets on the market for sprouting seeds, but you can use what you have on hand: a colander and white paper towels. The seeds should be bought from a health food store, not a nursery, where fungicide or other poisons may have been used for coating them.

Choose from alfalfa seeds, soy beans, Chinese mung beans, or wheat or rye seeds. Soak a few overnight in cool water and in the morning rinse and place on a layer of paper towel in the colander. Cover with another towel. Put the whole thing under the tap and soak everything. Let drain, then put aside in a corner of your kitchen counter. Repeat the soaking process each morning until the sprouts appear and are long enough. Except for alfalfa and mung beans, they should be about the length of the seed itself. This applies especially to wheat and rye, for the longer sprouts from these become too stringy to eat. Alfalfa and mung sprouts may be as long as you wish.

When the sprouts are ready, remove them to a plastic bag and refrigerate. They will keep about a week. Meanwhile start a new batch. DO NOT COOK THEM or you will destroy the auxins or rejuvenating substances. Use in salads, or in place of lettuce in sandwiches. Eat some daily as snacks or add at the last minute to soups and omelets – to warm only, not cook.

Another life-promoting food is the uncooked yolk of a fertile egg. A fertile egg hatches; an infertile egg does not. The raw fertile egg is the food from which the small chicken grows, yolk *and* white, and to which it owes its growth and existence. Some people insist that the white is useless. Some day we will find that again Nature knows best and put the white in the egg for a purpose. If you read that fertile eggs are no better for you than infertile eggs, remember that most large chicken-raising companies do not have fertile eggs to sell. A fertile egg requires the presence of a cock for hens who scratch and feed on the ground. Most chicken-raisers keep their chickens in wire cages. The hens never see the ground.

Protein

You have already read that protein is urgently needed in order to keep your body muscles firm and your body machinery working properly. If you have a protein digestion problem, you also know by now how to solve that problem. Check to see if you need HCL.

Brewer's Yeast

Brewer's yeast, sometimes called nutritional yeast, since it is no longer restricted to by-products of brewing but developed especially as a food, is one of our power foods. It contains most of the important B vitamins, all of the essential amino acids or protein factors (thus is a complete protein food), as well as the major minerals.

It is one of the greatest sources of energy available. People who take it feel a pick-up within about ten minutes, and it lasts several hours. It can be taken in water, juice, or broth. Most people begin gradually with one teaspoonful per day and work up to a tablespoonful. If gas develops, remember it is a high protein food (although it contains no animal products), and HCL can come to the rescue. It is even more powerful when taken with desiccated liver tablets. It comes in flakes or powder, is available at health stores, and because it contains so many nutrients is a bargain. The newer yeasts are far more palatable than the earlier varieties.

A New Source of Oxygen

There is a new, exciting yeast from Germany called *Zell Oxygen* (meaning cell oxygen). It is a liquid yeast containing billions of live yeast cells and enzymes, is formulated to deliver oxygen to tissues and organs, and is being used with success throughout Europe. According to German researchers, this yeast product stimulates the bioelectric potential as well as metabolism in the body.

This yeast is not the same as raw baker's yeast (which reportedly can steal B vitamins from the body via the intestines). In fact, according to researchers, these live yeast cells (not killed by heat) do not reproduce in the intestines, yet they do help restore damaged intestinal flora in a comparatively short time. The yeast is cultured at 86°F.

Zell Oxygen is available by mail from Bio-Nutritional Products, PO Box 389, Harrison, NY 10528, U.S.A.

(30°C.), substantially below body temperature. The culturing process is somewhat similar to the culture of live acidophilus. There are 5,000,000 living, nutritional yeast cells per 1/5th teaspoonsful.

Zell Oxygen differs from dry, regular brewer's yeast in that this liquid yeast contains live cells and enzymes, whereas dried brewer's yeast is inert from exposure to heat treatment. Zell Oxygen yeast is a form of primary yeast known as *Saccharomyces cerevisiae*, an excellent primary-source strain.

According to the German researchers, Zell Oxygen yeast contains B vitamins, minerals, and amino acids (also found in brewer's yeast), but the live elements in the yeast have been found to improve food assimilation, help regulate blood fats as well as digestion of fats, promote brain and nerve and liver function, improve circulation and help detoxify contaminants in the body from the many pollutants we are exposed to today. The liquid yeast, since it activates metabolism, is further enhanced by adding a B-vitamin complex product (as in tablets) to the diet, as well as coupling its use with exercise and deep breathing to encourage the increase of body oxygen to the highest possible level.

These statements about Zell Oxygen are not claims made by me or the distributors of this product, but are the research findings translated from the German scientific literature on the subject. These scientists have learned that as a result of taking this active yeast animals had a longer life span, a healthier nervous system, softer fur or more elastic skin, and exhibited higher levels of RNA-DNA in their tissues. Similarly, humans were found to develop a smooth juvenile skin, experience body strengthening and a feeling of well-being, with greater ability to concentrate and also both to fall asleep more easily and sleep the night through.

The Results

Here are some statements by European patients who have used Zell Oxygen:

One woman wrote: 'I began taking Zell Oxygen after a serious operation that caused much loss of weight. I have regained the weight and have continued taking Zell Oxygen for four and a half years. In spite of my eighty-two years, I feel very well and am doing my own housework.'

Another woman reported that she has been taking Zell Oxygen with buttermilk every morning for three years. (Some people take it with juice, others in plain water.) She says: 'I feel so young and vital that ten months ago I started doing housework for my son's four-member household, a task that lasts from 7.00 a.m. to 8.00 p.m. All my friends are enthusiastic about my appearance and performance. Though I am seventy-three years old, they tell me I look like a young woman.'

A man who suffered severe shortness of breath on climbing stairs reported: 'After taking three bottles of Zell Oxygen, I feel reborn.'

Zell Oxygen, largely because it is imported, is not cheap, but physicians believe that five bottles a year are sufficient to produce the therapeutic results desired.

Yogurt and Acidophilus

Yogurt and/or acidophilus can keep your intestines in order. Healthy intestines have what is called benign intestinal flora. These help you to manufacture certain B vitamins and discourage infections in the intestines. Unfortunately, antibiotics kill the intestinal flora, and indigestion may result. Yogurt, or acidophilus, which is stronger, helps to restore and maintain normal intestinal flora.

Yogurt has been credited with youth-giving qualities. It has been used constantly by inhabitants of Eastern Europe, noted for their longevity and excellent health. It has also been found to be a *natural* antibiotic, and it has recently been shown that it lowers excess cholesterol. Vanderbilt University has discovered that the Masai tribesmen, partly because of their high intake of yogurt, are virtually immune to heart disease. Most people have to learn to like yogurt. Try to cultivate the taste for the natural, plain variety instead of that mixed with sugar, jams, and other unmentionables. (Sugar can not only cause tooth decay and hypoglycaemia but also heart disease. If you cannot take yogurt because of milk intolerance, use one or more tablets of milk digestant (see Chapter 7) *before* eating yogurt.

Lecithin

Now for some dramatic news! As people get older their immunity system can weaken, making them more susceptible to infection. Vitamin C helps to forestall infections, but there is help against the virus problem and other disturbances by the use of lecithin. This information, which is almost earthshaking, was originally reported several years ago by Lester M. Morrison, MD, but nobody seemed to notice it.

As you have already read, Dr Morrison was apparently one of the first doctors to recognize that lecithin could emulsify or dissolve fat, and as he explains it: 'Apparently lecithin has the ability to increase the esterases in the human bloodstream. These esterases are enzymes that aid in the metabolizing of fat or cholesterol.'

But Dr Morrison goes much further. He says that *lecithin also has the ability to increase the gamma globulin in the body*. (Gamma globulins attack various infections.) Dr Morrison states: 'In the bloodstream of patients who used lecithin as recommended we found evidence of increased immunity against virus infections.' He points out that scientists have also reported that lecithin can produce immunity against pneumonia and prevent a variety of other diseases, including rheumatic carditis, liver diseases, anaemia, kidney disorders, and certain skin diseases, including psoriasis.

Others have noted lecithin's good effect on the brain. Lecithin is high in phosphorus. There is a saying, 'No phosphorus, no brains.' In addition, lecithin can act as a natural tranquillizer, since a high concentration of lecithin is found to occur in a normal body, not only in the brain, but in the myelin sheath surrounding the nerves, thus producing a natural tranquillizing effect. It is also normally present in the heart, the bone marrow, the kidneys, liver, spinal cord, and blood, as well as in glands, especially the sex glands.

Since it has also been reported to be helpful in dissolving gallstones, lecithin indeed has remarkable value for health. When an element is so widespread in the body, it is continually needed to maintain its level. So adding it to the diet regularly is an important precaution.

Edward R. Hewitt, a lecithin researcher, says: 'It must be well understood that lecithin is not a drug; it is a food. There is no danger in taking it. It simply furnishes some of the materials the body needs for growth and renewal of cells.'[2]

Dr Morrison concludes: 'Lecithin is one of our most powerful weapons against disease.' He found it took about three months to reverse many serious conditions due to its deficiency.

I have explained earlier what kinds of lecithin to take and how much. I take a tablespoonful of the liquid in fruit juice before breakfast, followed by a hot drink to help dissolve it. Liquid lecithin looks and pours like honey. Since it is sticky and clings to any container or spoon, I reserve a small empty jar for this use only. In the morning I add a tablespoonful or so of cold fruit juice to the jar, followed by an estimated tablespoonful of the liquid lecithin (to bypass a measuring spoon), and gulp down the whole thing directly from the jar. In a few days the lecithin will start to cling to the inner walls of the jar. This residue can be wiped out with a dry paper towel, or soaked and washed with liquid detergent plus water, or removed by both methods. An even less messy way is to swig it straight out of the bottle. I suggested it to one fastidious friend, and she swears by it.

I also add a heaping tablespoonful of lecithin granules to my protein drink, which I have for lunch. This consists of a cupful of juice (fruit or tomato) or yogurt, plus a heaping tablespoonful each of brewer's yeast as well as lecithin granules and perhaps a dash of desiccated liver powder.

Alan H. Nittler, M.D., the nutritional physician claims that lecithin alone has cured many cases of flu. *Warning*: Lecithin is high in phosphorus and can cause an acute calcium shortage if this high dosage is continued. (This often results in leg and other cramps.) If you need more than one series of six doses of lecithin for flu, be sure to add large quantities of calcium such as calcium lactate to offset the calcium loss. Dr Nittler summarizes: 'The lecithin routine can be used for any virus infection, such as measles, shingles, or chicken pox.'

The fact that women often live longer than men mystifies everyone. Years ago I came across an explanation that startled me and that I put in my book *Stay Young Longer*. Apparently nobody noticed it except one man, who told me he had read and followed the advice. He has already outlived other men his age. To my knowledge he is still following the advice. Greatly abbreviated, it is this:

Semen apparently contains lipoids, or phospholipids – mainly lecithin – which appear also in the brain and nerves. Doctors who have studied the subject found that seminal discharges can cause withdrawal of lecithin and its components from the body, depriving the arteries as well as sex glands, brain, and nerves of these substances, 'which are of utmost importance for its nutrition ... in other words the organism needs more incoming energy than leaves the body.' Therefore, lecithin must be put back in the body to compensate for the loss.

If lecithin is added to the male diet to replace its loss through semen discharge, there is apparently less danger of a deficiency developing. Since lecithin is found to exist in many other parts of the body as well as these crucial areas, perhaps by keeping it in the diet at all times to compensate for lecithin withdrawal via the semen, senility could be lessened, nerves fortified, and life lengthened. Every wife would do well to serve her husband lecithin, as well as vitamins A, E, and B daily to insure his health, youth, and longer life.

High Energy Multi-Purpose Food

There are many good protein powders on the market. They usually contain many high-powered foods: soya flour, alfalfa, lecithin, wheat germ (which contains vitamin E and protein), rice polishings (contain B vitamins), kelp (minerals), food yeast, plus B-12, as well as ground raw seeds – alfalfa, pumpkin (rich in zinc for skin, hair, and prostate), sesame, sunflower (rich in minerals, vitamins, and protein), flax (for skin and constipation), and Chia (for energy). This powder contains no animal products, salt, sugar, or preservatives.

Onions and Garlic

Onions and garlic are considered beneficial foods. Garlic has been found to be a help in lowering high blood pressure,[3] as well as discouraging parasites in people and animals. Doctors have fed onions and garlic to horses to reverse obstructions from atherosclerosis in the legs. Both onions and garlic contain sulphur, a blood cleanser. Garlic can be taken in pearl form. Garlic extract in liquid form has recently become available from health food stores, and this product leaves no unpleasant after-breath odour.

Recent reports show that garlic can be a rejuvenator too. In an article in *New Woman*, an American magazine (March-April, 1978), Rex Adams explains that garlic produces a tonic effect on all parts of the body: skin, muscles, tissues, nails, hair, organs, and bloodstream, even the hormone glands. Adams, also an author of a book on 'miracle foods', believes that garlic invigorates as well as rejuvenates. He claims this can happen within a surprisingly short time, helping you to turn the clock back in the way you feel as well as in the way you look.

The garlic diet suggested by Rex Adams is simple: a protein at every meal as well as garlic in some form. For breakfast, toast could be spread with garlic butter; at lunch and dinner chopped raw garlic can be added to vegetables or salad dressings. He says that if you don't like garlic or do not want to be socially unacceptable, you can use, instead of fresh, raw garlic, a garlic perle or capsule (from health stores) before each meal. It is said that eating a sprig or two of parsley after a meal containing garlic will destroy the odour, at least temporarily.

Adams reports that garlic increases circulation and oxygen, detoxifies the bloodstream, and, when used with leafy green vegetables, helps to release vitamins, minerals, and enzymes from other foods.

Salt Free Diet

In addition to a fat-free diet, many orthodox doctors are recommending a salt-free diet. Nutritionists frown on this practice. The body needs *some* salt, or sodium, otherwise disturbing problems can result. For example, the body requires some salt to manufacture HCL. Again, it is a matter of how much and what kind of salt. The average salt cellar on your table contains pure, refined sodium chloride. A whole natural salt includes many minerals in trace amounts. Using small amounts of salt may suffice, but its presence is still crucial!

There are available a few salts that are whole salts, meaning that they contain traces of many minerals, not just sodium chloride alone. *These whole salts taste and look the same as sodium chloride*, but are preferable in normal amounts to sodium chloride, taken alone. I use this whole salt exclusively and there are several types available in health stores.

Too little sodium in the diet can cause great fatigue. Remember the warnings of heat prostration for which doctors have actually prescribed salt? This deficiency can occur at other times in addition to heat exposure; many times great fatigue can be traced to a lack of sodium. Why? Doctors may have forgotten that salt is an important substance, which provides a base for producing electrolytes in the body. This, in turn, helps to generate body electricity, or energy. One nutritional physician tells his heart patients, whom he has first checked thoroughly, but who still may have intermittent feelings of weak pulse, to put some sea salt in a jar, add water, and sip whenever the weakness appears. This 'revs' up the body electricity and increases the heart's energy, as well as that of the body as a whole. Patients report remarkable relief. (This should be done under medical supervision.)

Do not be hoodwinked by a label on any container stating that a salt is sea salt. It is probably from the sea originally, but, in the process of drying, the pure sodium chloride may be precipitated out and other important trace minerals that are so valuable eliminated. Therefore, it may be a sea salt, but not a *whole* sea salt.

REFERENCES
(See *Bibliography* for fuller details.)

1. Linda Clark, *Stay Young Longer*.
2. ———, *Secrets of Health and Beauty*.
3. ———, *Handbook of Natural Remedies for Common Ailments*.

12

Other Aids to Rejuvenation

Minerals

Without minerals vitamins cannot work properly. Minerals are now considered by some even more important than vitamins. Both are necessary. Enzyme activity is also dependent on minerals.

Recent research by doctors and scientists indicates that minerals not only help to slow down ageing; they help you live longer, feel better, and look younger. These same researchers have learned that a lack of minerals can cause fatigue, sleeplessness, poor skin and muscle tone, vision problems, joint stiffness, and premature ageing.

John A. Myers, M.D., a mineral researcher of Baltimore, Maryland, U.S.A., calls attention to an article in *National Geographic Magazine* by Alexander Leaf, M.D., Chief of Medical Services at Massachusetts General Hospital and Professor of Medicine at Harvard University Medical School, who studied the incredible longevity of the Hunzas in a mountain recess of Kashmir, as well as of inhabitants of certain areas of Ecuador and Russia. Dr Leaf was convinced that the good health and longevity of these centenarians was due to a low-animal fat, low-cholesterol, low-calorie diet – *and* the liberal use of minerals in their agriculture and diet. Dr Myers says: 'It is my opinion that these people maintain their health and longevity from the activation of these mineral elements ...' Dr Myers has worked for years with minerals, and his word carries authority.

Mineral supplements, usually extracted from sea kelp, are available at health stores. Recent information suggests that minerals may be *the* primary anti-ageing factor.

Vitamins

Nutritionists believe you cannot eat enough of today's commercial foods to get the amount of vitamins and minerals your body needs to keep your cells in top condition. So you also need vitamin and mineral supplements. But you need not just one vitamin, you need *all* vitamins and minerals. In nature they do not occur singly but in combination. One helps another. Granville F. Knight, M.D., a nutrition-orientated allergist, says: 'Since food is not what it used to be, we are all nutritional cripples, and need vitamins and minerals as supplements.'

In general you need the B vitamins for your nerves, your hair, your skin, and your heart. You need vitamin E to bring oxygen to your heart and other muscles; it is considered a youth vitamin. Raymond F. Bock, M.D., a practising gynaecologist, states: 'Vitamin E is the vitamin most deficient in our diet.' Dr Bock agrees that vitamin E is a fertility vitamin. He uses it for menopause patients, heart problems, and fatigue. He says: 'It increases muscular efficiency, combats muscular fatigue, improves general circulation, and therefore circulation to the muscles.' He also finds that vitamin E helps alcoholics. He adds: 'With an adequate intake of vitamin E everyone will feel better, look younger, and live longer.'

Dr Knight claims that 'Vitamin E is essential for the reproduction of human cells.' Please study the section on vitamin E in my book *Know Your Nutrition* in order to learn what kind and how much to take. No two people need the same amount. Those who have had rheumatic fever or who have high blood pressure need to be cautious about taking too much. Otherwise you can feel your way, week by week, until you learn how much agrees with you.

Vitamin C is another oxygen carrier and helps you feel better as well as fight infection. Again, *Know Your Nutrition* gives you a safe guideline for its use.

Furthermore, I cannot tell you individually how much of each vitamin or mineral to take. First, I do not know. As already pointed out in Chapter 9 in discussing what foods *you* should eat, everyone is different. What might help me or your Aunt Emma would not be the right dose for you. Second, not being a doctor, I would not presume to prescribe or even recommend dosages. I can *report* on what appears in the literature, and that is as far as I dare go.

How to Take Supplements

The best thing I can advise is to use trial and error in your own case. Your body belongs to you, and you have the right to do with it what you will. Always take supplements at mealtime, not on an empty stomach. Start with low dosages, let a week or more pass before increasing them. But be sure to read first what to expect. You can do this in my *Know Your Nutrition*. Meanwhile, remember that you need everything, every day: raw foods, health-giving foods, all vitamins, all minerals, and plenty of protein, plus the digestive enzymes. This sounds like a big order, and it is. You really have to work at it, both by learning all you can about nutrition and then setting up your own programme. It is quite different from the early youthful years when cells build themselves more or less automatically, yet can steal nutrients from the rest of the body when they do not get them in your diet.

If you want to be well, healthy, and active, adopting a programme of good nutrition can be highly rewarding.

The Nucleic Acids: RNA-DNA

There is recent research on RNA and DNA, abbreviations for ribonucleic acid and deoxyribonucleic acid, chemical terms few people can pronounce or understand. The point is that RNA is being commercially promoted for use in the diet as well as on the skin in creams for cosmetic purposes to help reverse ageing. RNA is not something to play around with. If it is not used correctly (in oral doses), it can increase the body's uric acid, which nobody wants. Adding plenty of liquids and the B vitamin pantothenic acid helps somewhat, but I have talked with RNA research doctors, who prefer that you do not use this substance without medical supervision.

However, I have found for my own use, from many on the market, a type which is combined with several herbs. As each tablet contains approximately 50mg of RNA, though this is not stated on the label, it is presumably safe in this potency. Your health store may be able to offer advice here.

Helping Your Memory

Now for an exciting discovery for improving memory. A new product has become available and is causing excitement among those who are using it. It is a herbal extract made from a plant, a common ground cover, myrtle, or periwinkle (*Vinca major* and *Vinca minor*). Its value has been known since 1684. Recently a Frenchman, Dr Paul Coupan, researched it with many patients who were suffering from senility, with excellent results. In drug form it is now available as *Vincamine*, which, according to this doctor, has halted, even reversed, the ageing process in the brain, including dizziness, poor memory, bad temper, loss of concentration, and other symptoms of ageing. Dr Coupan, director of the Dausse Laboratories in Toulouse, France, states that *Vincamine* restores oxygen to the brain, loss of which is a prime cause of senility, and is said to halt the damage to the cells, therefore rejuvenating them.

Another French doctor, Louis Arbus, a neurologist at Pourpan Hospital in Toulouse, says: 'The drug lives up to the claims that are made for it.'

Still another, Dr George Duche of the French Convalescent Establishment in Paris, reports: 'We used *Vincamine* on 100 aged patients suffering from visual, hearing, and speech problems, dizziness, loss of memory, and mental disturbances. Nearly all benefited. It led to an improvement or total disappearance of the symptoms complained of.'

There is also a natural, safe and effective non-drug form of Vincamine which is the periwinkle extract with no chemicals added. People I know who use it report they can now remember names and other details they could not previously recall. One man could not even recall the names of people he had just met until he began taking periwinkle. Others who fell asleep in the midst of concerts or conversations (a common occurrence among older people) became alert once more.

Since this form of periwinkle is an herb, not a drug, it is well worth a try. It is not too expensive. Most people take five or more drops in approximately 10ml of water first thing in the morning. If they need more, they step it up gradually; some people need it twice daily, others do not. Taken at bedtime it can cause sleeplessness, since it encourages oxygen, thus wakefulness, to the brain at night, so taking it on an empty stomach in the morning may bring better results.

Refined and Adulterated Foods
There are various foods to avoid in your nutrition programme. Sugar, refined foods, foods with additives, colourings, preservatives (read your labels) do your cells more harm than good. There is no point in eating junk food just to fill your stomach. Make every bite count!

On the other hand, don't feel guilty if you are invited out and your hostess serves you such food. It isn't what you eat occasionally, but regularly, that counts.

Surveys show that improved nutrition can prevent 300,000 fatal heart attacks and strokes each year as well as millions of cases of respiratory infections, 150,000 deaths from cancer annually, and substantial reductions in mental illness, allergies, alcoholism, arthritis, dental problems, diabetes, digestive disorders, eye ailments, kidney disease, muscular disorders, and overweight.

Is it worth the effort to follow this new way of life? Indeed it is!

A Help for Nearly Every Need
If, after persistence in following the suggestions given to you to improve your health (which in turn helps to defeat ageing), you still have some nagging symptoms that refuse to disappear, there is one more thing to fall back upon: homoeopathy.

For those of you who do not already know about homoeopathy, it is a system of reversing illness without drugs, practised by some medical doctors who have elected to take training in its use. Because it is safe, cheaper, simple, and competitive with drugs, it has been belittled, and there have been attempts to stamp it out entirely. The few doctors who still practise it have often achieved miracles where ordinary drugs and other treatments have failed.

An excellent introductory guide is *Homoeopathy* by Dr A.C. Gordon Ross (See Bibliography). To find a homoeopathic doctor in your area, write to the British Homoeopathic Association, 27a Devonshire Street, London W1N 1RJ.

Food Substitution Chart

DO NOT EAT	DO EAT
cooked foods exclusively	sprouts; natural, whole, raw foods
bleached, salted nuts	nuts in shell, raw or home-roasted whole nuts
chemical imitation flavour	pure extracts
preserved mayonnaise	natural mayonnaise (homemade or natural foods store)
Ketchup, A-1 sauce, etc.	homemade sauces, Tamari, soy sauce
saturated fats, lards, oils, Crisco, vegetable oils, margarine, salad dressings	unsaturated, unrefined oils (corn, sesame, sunflower, safflower, olive, soy, peanut); dressings made from these; pure butter
ice cream	fresh fruit-flavoured yogurt
packaged, frozen, canned vegetables, fruits, soups	fresh fruits and vegetables in season; homemade soup; vegetable broth
Monosodium Glutamate (MSG) found in many canned and frozen foods, a commercial seasoning	dried herbs and herbal blends
dyed orange and processed cheeses	white raw cheese
baking powder, baking soda, preserved yeast	natural yeasts, living yogurt starters, unleavened products
chocolate, cocoa	carob and carob products
potato chips, corn chips with additives	natural corn, rice cakes, nuts and seeds
commercial red meats (read labels for nitrate, nitrite, and avoid)	fish, fowl, organic eggs, organic beef

AVOID REGULAR USE OF	SUBSTITUTE
sugar and sugar substitutes (including saccharin)	fresh and dried fruits, honey, date sugar, molasses, maple syrup, sorghum
milk (pasteurized, homogenized)	soya and nut milks, raw milk, goat's milk, yogurt, kefir
table salt (sodium chloride), iodized salt	whole sea salt, sesame salt, powdered kelp, sea-weed
tap water	tested spring, filtered water or mineral water
soda, coffee, tea	fruit juices, coffee substitutes, herbal teas
all commercial morning cereals	rolled oats, granola, oatmeal; whole, cracked, and flaked grain cereals
white bread	whole grain breads
white rice	brown rice and other grains
commercial peanut butter and other bread spreads	natural peanut butter, sesame butter, and other nut butters
jams, jellies, preserves	natural fruit butters, honey
crackers made with saturated fats and/or bleached flour	whole-grain crackers; wheat, rye, rice cakes
sweets, chocolate	dried fruit and nut bars; whole dried fruits
aspirin, antacids	herbal teas

(Reprinted with permission from the Bluegrass Organic Consumer Association)

OTHER AIDS TO REJUVENATION

Since one secret of homoeopathy's success is to find the exact substance (often a herb or other natural substance) that is compatible with your symptoms, it will take a true homoeopath quite a while to question you and learn what your symptoms are. You will really receive full personal attention, not a brush-off. That the results are well worth it is attested to by thousands who have been taking these tiny sweet homoeopathic pills, put dry on the tongue and swallowed without water. *And they are absolutely safe.*

However, if you do not have a homoeopathic doctor in your area, there is a method of helping yourself with this amazing method. You will find all the information you need in an excellent book called *A Doctor's Guide to Helping Yourself with Homoeopathic Remedies*, by James R. Stephenson, M.D. (see Bibliography). (The book also lists the homoeopathic pharmacies where you can purchase or order homoeopathic substances by mail. I keep an almost complete supply on hand for every emergency. These remedies are far cheaper than most drugs and can be a real life- (or illness-) saver.

Just this week I was struggling with some stubborn symptoms that had defied all other treatment. Like many other people, I had saved the best for the last. Finally, I got around to this homoeopathic book. I did some searching and studying for help for my stubborn symptoms, then took the appropriate remedies. In less than a week I was completely free of my ailments, though they had been bothering me for more than a year. (As I have said, I always learn the hard way. Had I turned to this method earlier, I could have recovered sooner). Homoeopathy has been known and used safely for hundreds of years.

13

Regular Exercise Can Rejuvenate You

Whenever the subject of exercise is raised, most people start yawning – they think exercise is boring, takes too much effort, and requires self-discipline. These people would rather sit still and let others do it. Meanwhile, the others may go to the opposite extreme. They huff and puff and try to get back into condition all of a sudden. Some, when they find they haven't made themselves over within two weeks, give up entirely. Others continue to huff and puff, cheating at times, overdoing it at other times. Neither method brings results.

Dr Herbert DeVries, Professor of Physical Education at the University of Southern California, says: 'We've proved that any normal, healthy older person can rejuvenate himself to some extent through carefully planned and controlled exercise.' The time spent is short, the rewards great. He states: 'People ranging from 52 to 87, doing one-hour workouts in a leisurely manner *only three times a week* experienced the disappearance of long-standing migraines, headaches, backaches, relief of joint stiffness and muscle pain; reduction of nervous tension and body fat; lowered blood pressure; improvement of heart and blood vessel function, and increases in arm strength.' There was also a 9.2 per cent increase in oxygen consumption after just six weeks.

Said Dr DeVries: 'The programme was a real eye-opener in terms of increased vigour and sense of well-being in the elderly who took part.' It is a well-known fact that high blood pressure (hypertension) can rise sharply, not only as a result of emotional tension, but with sudden physical exercise. However, if exercise is begun gradually and continued regularly, high blood pressure can be dramatically lowered by exercise alone.

Good Food and Exercise

Exercise need not be dull, as I will show you shortly. It can be easy and fun. But why is it so helpful? There are several reasons.

As previously explained, diet is of primary importance in building the cells, thus helping you to acquire and maintain good health. But you also need exercise to stir up the circulation and distribute all those goodies you eat to the various parts of your body where the cells are. As people get older, they move less, and their circulation slows down. Hippocrates said, 'What you do not use, you lose', and this applies to good circulation. It also explains the tottery gait, the stiffness, the cold hands and feet and other miseries of older age. The blood with its cargo of nutrients is just not getting there.

Another reason for exercise is that the lymph gland system, which contains body fluids to carry away waste, cannot move unless *you* move it. Exercise creates the necessary movement that carries away the body waste products, or 'clinkers', from the cells, thus speeding up their repair.

And of course the increased oxygen intake brought about by exercise is a must for the brain, muscles, heart, and other functions necessary for good health. Have you ever noticed how former athletes who give up exercising often become some of the paunchiest Seniors in later life? I personally know one of them.

This man was at one time a world champion wrestler who was handsome, well built, and lithe. As long as he was doing his thing athletically, he told me, his health was adequate in spite of a poor diet. But when he finally retired from the ring and gave up his regular exercise routine, his health went to pieces. He became a near-invalid. He was pain-ridden and looked fifteen years older than he was. Orthodox doctors, who tried drugs on him, said there was nothing they could do.

Fortunately, he learned about nutrition, improved his diet accordingly, and gradually rebuilt his health by diet alone, became handsome once more, and looked even younger than his age. The peculiar thing about this man is that with exercise alone, or diet alone, he was healthy. This should be a lesson for all of us. Why not build superhealth by using both?

Starting Gradually

Now, if you have decided that you will, after all, get out of that chair and start to exercise, take it easy! Weekend exercisers only have not infrequently met their doom. After being sedentary all week and going on an exaggerated exercise binge weekends, they have done too much too soon, sometimes with fatal results. One doctor told me that on the last hole on the golf course some players could not resist finishing, and often died of heart attacks as a result. According to their co-players, they did not listen to their own fatigue warnings before they pushed themselves relentlessly 'that last mile'.

So whatever the vigorous exercise you choose, whether jogging, some sport, gymnastics, even yoga, for that matter, start gradually. If you were a tennis buff in your early years, you should know it's a pretty strenuous game. Wait until your doctor says you have built up your strength, vitality, and heart function before you tackle it.

What Kind of Exercise?

I have some suggestions to offer, but recommend that you consider only something pleasurable to *you*. If you don't like bowling, for instance, you will merely tense up if you bowl. The idea behind exercise is to relax your muscles so that the circulation will flow, not be dammed up.

This applies to housewives too. They often claim they get enough exercise doing housework. Oh no they don't! I speak from experience. I hate housework, and it is anything but relaxing for me. There are a few women, though very few, who really seem to enjoy it. So unless polishing furniture and waxing floors is your idea of fun, cut the housework to the necessary minimum and instead walk, swim, garden, golf, or do anything else you enjoy. But don't clench your fists and tense your muscles and do your duty and kid yourself you're getting good exercise. It won't do you one iota of good.

A skipping rope is a favourite of some people. Sauntering leisurely through the woods or back roads, skipping or running now and then if and when you have the impulse to do so is particularly recommended. You can also stop and rest when you feel like it. Above all, you can return home whenever you wish. Don't set any deadlines. Do what comes naturally. Only keep off the main roads and as far away from them as possible. They carry too great a risk of picking up lead poisoning from car exhausts.

You could also try cycling. This is not for me, as I live on a steep hill. But another of its suggestions revolutionized my life. It stated that regular exercise, including cycling, can decrease fat levels in the blood and that *a stationary bicycle is a good substitute for a moving bicycle*. So I bought an exercycle. It is the kind that works not only on your legs and lower part of your body by pedalling, but has handlebars and a seat that goes back and forth like rowing a boat, which exercises your upper body as well.

For those who suffer from high blood pressure there is further good news. Tests showed that regular exercise for seven months reduced the blood pressure of those who already had a high reading, and that exercise can help the condition at any stage.

What happens when you exercise regularly, experts explain, is that new blood-flow pathways are opened up, carrying fresh blood to the heart and other organs. With exercise gradually increased, the heart can develop more strength.

One warning: Whatever type of exercise you adopt on a regular basis, once you start, don't be wishy-washy about it. If you decide to take a day off, then two, then three, you have broken the habit, and it is hard to get with it again.

Dr David Kakiashvili, a Russian heart and gerontology (ageing) specialist, states that exercise is a major influence in longevity. He has learned that people who live in small mountain villages have fewer heart attacks than those who live in cities. Their way of life necessitates constant physical activity, which improves heart function and supplies more oxygen to the body than is the case of city dwellers with their far less physically active lifestyle.

Isometric Exercises
I have one other easy-does-it exercise to suggest. It brings oxygen to your muscles, which also include cells, and even if

one is bedridden, it can be done by anyone, no matter at what age or stage of decrepitude. It also takes less than three minutes. (This leaves you with no alibi for not exercising.) I call this method Muscle Massage (MM). It is actually a tranquillizer.

I received a clue to this method when I read that Dr Arthur Steinhaus, a former dean of physiology at George Williams College, had said: 'In a German laboratory where I worked, it was discovered that a muscle can grow only at a certain rate, and a small amount of the right exercise will start it growing at that rate. If you contract any one of your muscles to about one third of its maximum power and hold it for six seconds a day, the muscle will grow as fast as it can grow.'[1] This is admittedly an isometric exercise, considered by many ineffective. But good results are possible.

Where there are muscles, there are cells. Some of our muscles are voluntary, meaning we can move them; and others, on the inside of our bodies, are involuntary, meaning that we cannot control them at will. These would include our heart, glands, and some other organs. Even so, our bodies are really not compartmentalized. Each area nudges another, so that when we exercise the voluntary muscles, the involuntary muscles are also indirectly affected. So here's how you do it:

While you are lying in bed, in a bathtub, or sitting upright, you can tense and relax each area of your body.

— Begin with your toes. Squeeze them and bend them under, away from your body, and keep them clenched while you *slowly* count to six. This adds up to six seconds. (Say one hundred one, one hundred two, etc., up to one hundred six to slow down your counting.)
— Next bend your toes toward your body by bending your ankles. Your toes will not be clenched in this position. Hold for six slow counts.
— Now place your hands on top of your legs, between ankles and knees. Tense these areas for six counts. Use your hands to help locate the areas to be tensed. They are temporary spot finders. Later you may not need them.
— Place your hands under your calves and repeat.
— Now place your hands on your knees and tense.
— You are ready for your thighs. Put your hands first on top

for six slow counts, then underneath thighs, and tense accordingly.
- Next, tense your buttocks; count to six.
- The next area is a little harder. Sit up if you are lying down, reach behind you, place your palms on your back just above your waistline and on either side of your spine. This is the kidney and adrenal area (there are two of each), each set on either side of your spine. Try tensing or pushing those areas against your hands. Count to six as usual.
- Return to the front of your body for three more areas here. Contract your stomach muscles, then your rib cage, and then your chest (which houses your lungs, heart, thymus). Push each area against your hands, counting six slow times for each. Do not hurry.
- Your shoulders will take a bit of doing too. Put one hand on the opposite shoulder, hunch your shoulder, and tense. Repeat with the other one.
- Clench your hands, then the lower arms, then the upper arms. Count six for each.
- Place your hands on the front of your neck, then on the sides, and finally at the back of your neck, in each position tensing to six counts, then relaxing. Great tension can accumulate in the neck. (These neck tension positions help firm the neck and smooth away some of that flabby look.)

Additional Exercises

Since you need extra relaxation here, an additional exercise is invaluable at this point. Use the head roll exercise. Sit up straight, stretch your neck, and keep it that way. Now roll your head slowly in a complete circle, three times to the right, three times to the left. This also helps circulation reach the face, the eyes, ears, even the scalp.
- Clench your teeth and jaws. Count six.
- Put your hands on your cheeks and tense, then on your forehead, ditto.
- Now, *very important*, take your two index fingers and place lightly on each eye. Tense each eyeball. Repeat twice for the count of six, especially if your eyes are weak.
- Finally, spread your fingers apart, lay them on top of your head, bracing them with your thumbs placed behind your

ears. Now pitterpatter your fingers all over the top of your head. You will be amazed at the circulation you detect in your head as you finish. This does not require counting.
— Most important of all, now do the all-over clench. Stand up, if possible, and slightly flex your knees and your elbows. Tense your entire body, holding for the same count of six.

The all-over clenching routine is absolutely safe. It was developed by two doctors to reduce high blood pressure. There were no side effects and nothing but good results noted in all people tested.[2] Blood pressure dropped when it was high.

If you do not believe this MM routine takes less than three minutes, time it! Do it once daily.

Since more vigorous exercise helps to reduce blood fat, add some other more active exercise of your choice. Watch out for indiscriminate jogging without your doctor's advice. Reports are accumulating that doing too much too soon can be dangerous. Again, let your heart become accustomed to exercise gradually. Never overexert at any stage.

A Surprising Secret of Health

Recently a new secret of a cause of illness and pain made its appearance in our country. This may well shake up the whole world before long. Various world cultures have always believed that there is a vital force within our bodies. English-speaking scientists and others call it *Life Force*. The Hindus or Indian Yogis call it *Prana*. The Chinese call it *Chi*. Other peoples have other names for it.

One theory is that *all illnesses and pain are the result of the interruption of the flow of the vital force in the body*.

This surprising and simple concept may explain the success of many therapies. Acupuncture needles are inserted at certain body points to release the congestion there and elsewhere in the body. Acupressure, which uses finger pressure instead of needles, has the same effect. If you do not believe this, investigate for yourself by pressing your fingers against the various spots of your body considered key points by acupuncturists and acupressurists. If you find a sore spot, it indicates, according to experts in the subject, that there is a congestion relating to some organ or gland in the body. *And it works.* Either by the insertion of needles or by pressure of the finger (the latter repeated daily for a short period) the soreness or congestion disappears, and the area to which the congested spot is linked responds likewise. This release of congested life force at various points could also be the explanation of reflexology, which is actually acupressure on the soles of the feet. It may also explain the success of Chiropractic and Osteopathy, through which certain nerve impingements are released, thus, in turn, restoring circulation of the interrupted flow of vital force in the body. No doubt osteopaths and chiropractors, and also some highly trained massage therapists, have always known this.

The relaxing method I call MM, described previously, can also remove interruption and congestion of the flow of the body's vital force. If you decide to try reflexology of the feet, you can follow the direction in any book on the subject and achieve results similar to those of acupressure. My favourite reflexologist is Anna Kaye, who has written a book with Don C. Matchan about it called *Reflexology: Techniques of Foot Massage for Health and Fitness.* (Thorsons Publishers Ltd. 1979).

Non-Exercises

Once you form the habit of learning and using the MM plan, as well as the method of massaging sore spots in your body, you will no doubt feel more relaxed and normal. But if you want to try something still more unusual and equally effective – which helps rejuvenation as well as general health – you can use the system of *internal exercises*, another little-known exciting method of self-healing.

Some strenuous exercises can be dangerous for some people, whereas it is thought that internal exercises, which are more passive, are safe. They are designed to energize the whole body, balance the energy level, promote better functioning, and regulate the action of the internal organs, as well as liberate the flow of Chi (vital force).

Internal exercises can:
— reduce high blood pressure

— improve vision and hearing
— reduce the size of your stomach
— overcome male impotence
— increase energy
— reduce or remove wrinkles and many more.

I can give you three rejuvenating-type exercises which have been known and practised for more than six thousand years, yet are virtually unknown in the Western world. These exercises are based on observations of three animals noted for their longevity: the deer, the crane and the turtle. Here's a short, condensed version of each.

The Deer

The deer, if you will watch it in action, waves its short tail back and forth constantly, which in turn activates and recharges, stimulates and strengthens the sexual and other glands. The human version of this exercise does the same for humans, and also strengthens the anus, prostate, and vagina, which may tend to become flabby in later years.

The deer exercise is simple, and you can do it anywhere without being noticed. Merely tighten the anal (rectal) muscles and pull upward as hard as you can and hold as long as possible. This exercise is thought to generate new energy all the way up to the head and to the glands located there. Although once a day is sufficient, first thing in the morning and just before going to bed are especially helpful times to practise this exercise. Or you can do it as you sit at your desk or table, walk across the room, or stop at a stop light while driving.

The Crane

The crane exercise is devised to help the abdominal area (including relieve constipation), as well as stimulate the lungs, circulatory system, aid indigestion, and promote a flow of oxygen.

For a shortcut here, emulate the crane, which stands on one foot, folding its other leg into its belly. While you are doing this, first on one leg and then on the other (hold onto a chair or the wall if you need to maintain your balance), inhale and exhale deeply.

The Turtle
The turtle is well known for its longevity and performs only one major exercise – stretching its neck forward and pulling its chin inward toward the base of the neck, again and again. This exercise releases neck tension, as well as tension of the brain. It can also stretch the entire spine, energize the neck, strengthen the shoulder muscles, removing tiredness and soreness, and help to stimulate the thyroid, which is thought to increase energy and help you feel younger.

T'ai Chi

There is another type of exercise related to internal exercises that is more complex but very rewarding. It cannot be learned without a teacher, but is useful for everyone and can be started at any age. It is called T'ai Chi (pronounced Tye Chee), and to watch the slow, graceful movements of those who have learned how to do it is almost like watching ballet. The movements are slow, rhythmical, graceful, fluid, and beautiful. It appears to be effortless, can be done in ten minutes daily within a space of four feet, and without spending a cent once it is learned. The Chinese believe that if you do T'ai Chi twice a day regularly and correctly, in time you will develop the pliability of a child, the health of a lumberjack, and the peace of mind of a sage.

So if an instructor in T'ai Chi comes to your area, by all means join the class!

Although T'ai Chi is newer to the Western world than Yoga and, once learned, is considered by many students easier to perform, the practice of Yoga may be more satisfactory and helpful to most people. The Yoga asanas, or postures, are not aimed at performing acrobatics, as many people seem to think, but are devised to relax certain centres in the body and aid the interrupted pranic flow. They require less training to learn than T'ai Chi, and inexpensive classes are more widely available in small communities as well as in large cities.

According to recent findings Yoga can accomplish many things for those in their later years. Its practice has improved or reversed:
— stiffness
— respiratory ailments, including emphysema

— high blood pressure
— lack of muscle strength
— accumulation of fat in the wrong places
— back pain
— heart problems
— prevention of senility in some cases
— arthritis

and other afflictions.

Now for a source of more oxygen and stress relief.

REFERENCES
(See *Bibliography* for fuller details.)

1. Linda Clark, *Stay Younger Longer*.
2. Linda Clark, *Handbook of Natural Remedies for Common Ailments*. See chapter on High Blood Pressure.

14

Breathing for Health

Breathing should be automatic, and during sleep it usually is. But often during the daytime tense people unconsciously constrict their breathing or hold their breath, actually forgetting to breathe. You should check yourself at intervals. Lift your chest, drop your shoulders, then stretch the back of your neck (two common tension areas), and also check to see that you are breathing normally instead of holding yourself tense. If you are holding yourself tense, do some regular rhythmic breathing, choosing from any of the following methods. Breathing encourages more oxygen to the various parts of the body. It can also relieve tension or stress.

Captain N.P. Knowles, a breathing expert, says: 'When you feel signs of ageing, and wonder if there is anything you can do about it, there is one way: breathe.'

Captain Knowles, who has rehabilitated many students through correct breathing, explains that as we get older there is a tendency to worry about trifles. This creates nerve tension, which, in turn, restricts the supply of oxygen. He has found that by daily practice of better breathing we can send a fresh supply of oxygen to the brain and ease the tension.

Here is the method:

'Sit in an easy chair and gently draw your shoulders slightly backward. Relax your arms and hands: then breathe out gently as if in a long sigh.

'Then, as though smelling a flower, gently breathe in, pausing a second to allow the breath to be converted into oxygen in the lungs, then slowly and gently breathe out again.

'Pause a second to allow the carbon dioxide in the blood to be exhaled. Repeat this breathing method 12 times and you will be surprised at how different you feel. Why? Because you have given Nature a chance to recharge your system.'

If you do this simple exercise at the end of the day, Captain Knowles says, it will disperse fatigue.

The following method is used by Caryl Hill, who works with Seniors on the Monterey Peninsula in California. The Seniors are enthusiastic about the results. Here is the method she teaches these willing students:

Step One. Lie on the floor or a firm bed. Place one palm on your abdomen just below your navel. Place the other palm on your chest, close to the hollow of your neck.

Step Two. Take a deep breath through your nose. As you do this, your lower hand should (if you are breathing correctly) be pushed upward. Feel this breath roll upward through your lower and upper lungs to your other hand, which should go downward or inward or sideways.

Step Three. Exhale, slowly through your mouth, making any sound you wish – a groan, a hum, or whatever you feel like doing. This is a good way to relieve tension.

Caryl Hill explains that for best results there is a rhythm to follow in this exercise. Count 4 as you roll the breath upward, count 4 as you pause, exhale to the count of 4, then rest to the count of 4. (Later you may wish to work up gradually to the count of 8 for each step.)

Repeat the whole sequence seven times.

After learning how this feels while you are lying down, you can do the rhythmic breathing while standing, and then while walking. Some of the Seniors who live in a retirement centre reported that they had had difficulty walking from their rooms to the dining hall. However, by using this method as they walked, they reached the dining room with ease, plenty of energy, and without stopping.

When you get up out of a chair and start somewhere, even to the mailbox or bathroom, begin breathing as you walk. Deep breathing not only helps your circulation, it feeds oxygen to every cell through the bloodstream, combats poisons in the body, and increases mental alertness. So make a daily habit of breathing deeply. If you don't have time or inclination to count, merely breathe deeply and often throughout the day.

My own favourite breathing method for situations like these

is to breathe in deeply, then exhale through the mouth like a soundless whistle.

Yoga Breathing

Suza Norton an author on Yoga, gives some exciting results of Yoga breathing as well as easy-to-follow directions on how to do it. Here are some of the impressive things she suggests about breathing:

'Most people, young and old, use only one-third of their breathing capacity ... This continuous inadequate supply of oxygen to the body accelerates the ageing process, gradually impairing the functioning of vital organs.'

'Through the years slouching in chairs, overeating, work, and other tensions prohibit the complete and efficient use of the lungs.'

'Slow, even, complete breathing is more conducive to a feeling of vitality than almost any other single factor.'

'When you learn to slow down your breathing consciously, there is less wear and tear on the entire body – less work for the heart, lower blood pressure, and a general soothing of body tensions.'

'Breathing habits are really easier to change than eating habits, but just as important to your health.'

You really owe it to yourself to apply this information to help you breathe properly, which is a giant step toward rejuvenation.

A New Find

One of the world's greatest fears is ageing. People will succumb to any advertising, any gadget, any product, even surgery, if it will promise them protection from ageing. Actually, there is no single panacea for ageing (with the possible exception of one approach I will describe in the final chapter). So do not allow yourself to be gullible about it.

There are, however, various honest methods that may help. I have included them in this book. I refuse to discuss or even mention anything that might conceivably be a hoax, or a con game, and thus another disappointment to a person who tries something with great hope, only to find it is a dud.

I have recently found something new, which I have spent

much time in researching and which I feel has promise. In fact I am using it myself. Laboratory tests show that it can help people at any age, particularly those in later life. This 'find' is a machine known as a 'negative ionizer'.

In certain parts of the world at various times certain types of winds blow that cause all manner of discomfort – mentally, emotionally, and physically. People may become irritable, even violent or suicidal, under the influence of these winds. There is the *Foehn* in German and Switzerland; the *Mistral* in southern France; the *Hamsin* in the Middle East; the *Chinook* in the Pacific Northwest of the United States; and the *Santa Ana* in southern California.

The effects of these winds on people can be so disastrous that some doctors refuse to operate just before or during the time they are blowing, and judges are more lenient toward crimes and traffic accidents occurring at such times.

Years of study finally revealed that these winds produce electrical charges known as positive ions, which seem to be responsible for the disturbances felt by people. When the winds cease and the atmosphere is tranquil again, negative ions take over and calm is restored.

As a result of this scientific research, negative ionizing machines, after having been banned over twenty years ago because of claims benefiting a long list of physical and emotional disorders, are again becoming available. You cannot keep a good thing down forever, however, and the negative ionizers are back on the market, but with the warning to manufacturers that they must be called air cleansers, about which no medical claims are allowed.

Before I tell you the list of disorders negative ions are reported to have helped, you may have experienced them yourself in nature. There are high concentrations of negative ions on mountaintops, as well as close to the beach where the waves crash. A waterfall or running, splashing shower can produce negative ions. It is interesting that some of the longest-lived, healthiest centenarians live in mountain villages. The best most of us can do is to vacation in the high mountains or relax on the beach near the waves during an annual vacation. A negative ionizer changes all this. You can have the ions in your own home at the twist of a dial.

Beneficial Effects

What do the ionizers accomplish? I will list below the benefits reported, with their sources. This is strictly *reporting* and in no way intended to make medical claims.

Negative ions have been helpful for:
— tranquillizing and insomnia
— hay fever, bronchitis, sinus, asthma, and emphysema
— depression, tension, even suicidal tendencies
— use in hospitals for speeding healing of postoperative conditions as well as burns
— aching joints
— fatigue
— delivery of more oxygen to various tissues of the body (so necessary to the ageing), with improved mental efficiency and many other benefits.

No danger or side effects from natural or machine-made negative ions have ever been found.

You may contend that you do not live in an area where winds producing high positive ions blow. Perhaps not. But positive ions can be generated by other causes in our environment than these disturbing winds. Air conditioning and machinery, such as cars and planes, can generate positive ions leading to positive ion poisoning. So can synthetic fabrics in clothes, carpets, and furnishings, as well as cigarette smoke.

I turn my ionizer on in my bedroom and sleep with it running (it is quiet) *every* night, *all* night. A friend of mine who suffers from emphysema wrote to me recently saying that he detected no improvement in his chest condition after using the ionizer. 'But', he added, 'I do not remember to turn it on except occasionally.' No wonder! Until symptoms are under control, the effect of an ionizer is noticeable only after continuous use, not a now-and-then use. As an extra bonus, my ionizer completely cleans the air in my room three times every hour and does away with household or cooking odours in a very short time. I am now planning to buy a portable ionizer to carry with me in my car or in transit when I travel by other means.

Negative ionizers (or air cleansers) are available from Medion, Ltd., Box 1, Oxted, Surrey.

15

Changing Your Life Through Thought

Feeling left out, or on your own, or ignored by others is sometimes a Senior's own fault. It is always easier to blame others for your misfortune than to face up to your own weaknesses. But at this time of life it is crucial to set up your new way of life in such a way that you attract others instead of repelling them.

Because many ageing people may be depressed at the death of a mate, or loss of a job or status of some kind – or because they may have let their health slip and do not feel well – they become cranky, crotchety, rigid, complaining, faultfinding, instead of flexible. Obviously this is not the route to popularity. Such negative attitudes scare away everybody except those who are forced to stand by to care for the ageing person, whereas they would rather flee or hide.

But there are also parents who act like martyrs, believing that since they gave their all to their children, their children should give their all to them. Worse yet is the parent left behind by the death of a mate, who transfers dependence from a departed husband or wife and clings to or commandeers their children, preventing them from making a life of their own. If these juniors try to achieve independence, the parent, perhaps unconsciously, stages a rage, pours out tears of recrimination, or manages a heart attack or some other psychosomatic ailment to obtain the abject submission of a son or daughter or a whole family of children.

I know an attractive, highly successful professional woman who lost her husband by death. She has substituted her son in many ways for the departed husband. The son is required to wait on her hand and foot, give up his own friends and interests in order to serve his mother's demands according to her constantly changing whims.

Another overlooked fault in many Seniors is not having anything to look forward to. All too often they live in the past, monopolizing the conversation with accounts of past deeds and successes, even old jokes, repeating them again and again to the intense boredom of any captive audience. This, of course, is due to lack of attention or a feeling of insecurity on the part of the Senior, who is trying to shore up his or her own ego or status that has slipped. Obviously, this habit can alienate everyone within earshot.

Cultivating Friends

Fortunately, not all Seniors are so thoughtless or selfish. Nor do they need to be. Better to be cheerful, develop a pleasant sense of humour, be a good listener, and show genuine interest in the problems of others. As a result, friends and relatives can be attracted to them as bees to honey, even though these same Seniors may be suffering emotionally. Wisely, they have decided that there is nothing to be gained by unloading their sorrows on others or wallowing in self-pity. So they have deliberately substituted a cheerful façade to present to the public. Even people who are pain-ridden or blind have proved to be highly popular, full of infectious good spirits, so that they cheer up those who need it. The secret here is that these individuals are full of love for others instead of self-love, are never critical or complaining. They thereby acquire charm and are beloved by others. Just remember that there is always some good in everyone if you look for it. Do not let anyone leave your presence without saying something good about whoever it may be. As has been said: 'Give him roses before he dies; don't wait until afterward; then it is too late.'

And do you know what? People who started out as disagreeable and deliberately acted agreeable have eventually *become* agreeable! This is because they have programmed their computer, which is giving out what they put into it.

Positive Thinking

Scientists have recently discovered a breakthrough in the control of the mind over the body. It is so rewarding that it can become the most fascinating game you ever played. You can get anything you want if you just learn the rules of how to programme your computer correctly. You can be well instead of sick, happy instead of sad, vital and energetic instead of weak, and wealthy instead of poor. There is practically no limit except for possibly not being able to grow a new limb. But you can programme your life so that it is better than ever before.

I could write a book full of other examples of people who have done it, but I'll give you one quick example before telling you how you can do it too.

One woman I am proud to call a friend is in her late seventies. She has been widowed, endured much suffering, including several near-fatal ailments. Yet she devotes her life to helping others, is now happily married to her second husband, is surrounded by countless admirers, who are so attracted to her that they follow her wherever she goes, basking in her radiance and love, which she bestows on all alike. She is truly beautiful inside and out. This adulation is deserved, because she has earned it through her own efforts to forget herself and help others unselfishly with their problems.

In order to change your life for the better through thought control the secret is that our subconscious mind soaks up, without logic or reasoning, whatever we think and feel, right or wrong. It acts exactly as a computer, putting out what is put into it. If you think sickness, sooner or later your subconscious will attract it! If you think poverty, the same thing happens. But if you think health or happiness *consistently*, that is what will become manifest, sooner or later. You can depend upon it.

You may say, 'Oh, I've tried that. It doesn't work for me.' The reason may be that you decided to be cheerful for one day and let sadness take over the next. Your computer (the subconscious) first gets the message 'cheer,' then, just as it is getting to work to follow instructions, you give it a countermessage of 'sadness', which cancels out the first message. This jams the works, and nothing at all happens! In other words, *you are what you think*. But there is a little trick here: You can add feeling to speed the action of the subconscious, as well as supply a visualization blue-print picturing whatever you wish (which shouldn't be changed every ten minutes or every day). You may have to fake the feeling you desire at first and try to feel healthy or cheerful even if you aren't. Pretty soon the idea will be picked up by your subconscious slave, and it will do your bidding.

Here is an example of another friend.

She too is radiant, joyful, happy, and loving, and attracts unlimited friends and followers. But I was surprised when she told me she was not always that way. She has had one of the most tragic lives I ever heard of, but she suddenly realized that the negative conditions in her life were not improving, but worsening. So one day she made a firm decision: From that day forward she would not think a negative thought or speak a negative word, no matter how strong the temptation.

Controlling the Subconscious

It was not an easy change. The subconscious does not like change and becomes grumpy, trying to pull you back into your old ways, because it is an easier, lazier way. But my friend, who is in her late sixties, was determined. Soon the fight was over, and she had won. Through constructive thinking she made herself *feel* cheerful and happy, though just the opposite was true at first. What could the subconscious computer do, other than balk, but obey? Sometimes you have to get pretty stern with your subconscious and talk to it in no uncertain terms. Many people give their subconscious a name, like Charles or Vivian. You may have to say firmly, 'Now listen, George, stop this nonsense. I want action NOW! I want you to ...' giving the command you expect to have followed. You may have to do it at least three times at one sitting to make sure the message gets through; and if you are not wishy-washy, but firm, it *will* get through.

At any rate, the affairs of my friend began to turn in the right direction. After being tragically widowed twice, she now attracted an adoring mate, and in many other ways she is truly happy, one of the best examples of computing I know.

In addition to consistent input of ideas, firmness, and feeling the way you want to feel (even though the desired condition hasn't yet manifested), the subconscious also likes pictures. It helps get the idea across faster. I have tried this myself many times with surprising results.

For example, I may have a desk piled high with unanswered

letters I dread doing, so I use the visualization method. I form a picture of the desk clean as a whistle, seeing myself feeling happy that I have finished the job. Then I put it out of my mind and forget it. (A watched pot never boils.) Some time later, when I least expect it, I suddenly feel just like doing the job, and turn to it with eagerness. In no time, it seems, it has gone speedily without any hang-ups, and the job is done. My desk is as clear as I envisioned it, and I feel as happy as I had wished.

Think Your Way to Health
This can be done with health too. You can visualize yourself looking and feeling well until you *do* feel well. Don't dwell on it or how it will come about in the meantime; this only delays it. Let the subconscious know what is needed and ask it to bring it to you. I never cease to marvel at what can happen. Sometimes I find that I may need a certain food or vitamin or something else to help my progress. It often takes time for the subconscious to discover this and bring it to you. But keep at it and the necessary help will come.

Warning: If you are not sure that something is right for you — say a certain job, or a mate, or a house — you had better qualify your demand with the statement, 'according to the will of God', or you might get something you later regretted.

Dr Venice Bloodworth is a trained counsellor in helping others, who testifies that her 'computing' method has changed many lives. She writes:

'Like attracts like. Whatever you hold in mind any length of time MUST come into expression for you.'

'Some people reap what they sow: failure — because they do not stick to their goal. Decide what you want and stick to it.'

'To have health, you must concentrate on health; to be loved, you must first love others; to have abundance, you must think abundance. Ignore the present conditions and hold fast to your new mental picture.'

She urges you to concentrate on what you want, *not on what you do not want*. Thoughts of discord, worry, envy, fear will be set in motion, sooner or later, bringing on those exact conditions. You cannot afford to harbour them for a minute! Do not forget, too, to avoid fear of *anything*. Since this is a magnetic *feeling*, as the Bible says, 'What you fear will come upon you.' But so will any other strong positive feeling bring *good* results. As Dr Bloodworth concludes: 'The magic secret of attainment is intense desire. Fix one goal at a time and concentrate on it exclusively.'

You can use little helps to keep up your courage while the changes you have computed are going through the incubation stage, before they appear. No doubt you remember that old motto of Coué: 'Every day in every way I am getting better and better.' It has worked for thousands who have used it consistently.

You can amend this to suit your needs, and chant it to yourself as you walk: 'Every day in every way I am getting healthier and healthier,' or 'I am becoming healthy, youthful, and loving,' or whatever you wish. Just press the right word button with force and repetition, and you can reshape your life as you want it to be.

16

Advice for Special Senior Problems

Your Feet
Since zones on the bottoms of your feet reflect areas throughout the entire body, it is not surprising that when your feet ache, you may ache all over. There are books on reflexology[1] to help you learn what is wrong with your feet as well as your body. Not only can you locate clues on the bottoms of your feet, but even though you do not have a book or foot chart, here is what you can do to obtain relief:

Explore, with your fingers, every inch of the bottoms of both feet, even under and around your toes, pressing firmly as you go. When you locate a sore spot, this is a sign of foot congestion, also linked to some congested area in the body. For example, your liver, or kidney, and other organs and glands are represented in some spot (or nerve ending) on your feet.

To correct, for a few seconds every day gently massage the sore spots with your fingertips to help break up the congestion until the soreness disappears. You may be surprised at the results, though they are not necessarily instantaneous. You will see by case histories in some of the books on the subject that many people have experienced near-miracles through reflexology.

How many women, after a shopping tour, can hardly wait to get home to kick off their shoes? That is probably because they are wearing the wrong type of shoes. We shudder at the Orientals who formerly bound the feet of their women to keep them small and dainty. But we think nothing of trying to squeeze our own feet into shoes manufactured for the 'average' person.

I recently read of a young man with one foot size 10 and the other foot size $8\frac{1}{2}$ who could not get one pair of shoes to fit both feet, so he took to making his own shoes for comfort. Nearly all of us have one foot larger, yet the smaller foot slides around in the size chosen to fit the larger foot, or the larger foot is constricted by the smaller size for vanity's sake. As for platform soles and heels, or stiletto heels, they can be forms of torture. The spine and posture are tipped out of alignment, and the whole body, as well as the feet, suffers. What area reflects this suffering first? Your face! No wonder our young people are rebelling and reverting to bare feet or sandals.

Fortunately, there are a few ready-made 'natural shoes' available today. Some people prefer one type; others like another. My favourite is called the *Birkenstock* footprint sandal, which feels as if you are making your own footprints in wet sand. The blessed relief that comes from wearing these sandals is almost incredible. Leg aches, backaches, foot aches have disappeared in men and women, and a feeling of buoyance results.

The footprint sandal is not pretty, but it is beginning to be considered 'smart'. You can wear it for walking, working, gardening, shopping, and casual wear, and reserve your dress shoes for special occasions only. I could not manage without mine. *Birkenstocks* are made in Germany, and no more expensive than ordinary dress shoes. And oh, what comfort! One pair outlasts several pairs of cheaper, shoddier sandals.

Leg and Other Cramps

People of all ages often become frightened when they suffer from leg cramps. Except for swimming cramps, a cramp is usually nothing more serious than a mild deficiency of certain nutrients and can soon be corrected permanently, perhaps in several days, so that it will not return.

The most common cause of leg or other cramps in the extremities is a shortage of calcium. These cramps may occur in the legs at night, and in the hands, fingers, or even in the upper ribs (where they may be mistaken for a heart attack) during the day.

Taking sufficient calcium may still not rid you of the cramps if it is not assimilated. Vitamin D (400 units a day in tablet form) is needed for calcium assimilation. Or a lack of acid in the system can also cause cramps. Calcium needs acid to dissolve it in the bloodstream so that it can be properly assimilated instead of piling up in the joints, where it is not wanted. Those who drink quantities of milk for calcium may still be deficient, since milk calcium may not be properly assimilated as one grows older. A surer way is to take calcium lactate or calcium gluconate tablets (available at drug and health shops). These forms of calcium are among the easiest to assimilate. But check your acid intake too. If necessary, add HCL to your diet, or sip apple cider vinegar in water to taste with your meals. Too much lecithin, taken over a prolonged period, can also produce a calcium deficiency and result in cramps. This is because lecithin is rich in phosphorus, which has a close affinity for calcium and is excreted with it from the body. The solution is not to avoid lecithin, a superior product, but to increase the calcium intake to make up for the deficit if you find you are having leg or other cramps.

A deficiency of B_6 has also been known to cause cramps in the calves of the legs.

If a cramp attacks while you are in bed, lie on your back and point your toes toward the ceiling until the cramp passes. If this fails, stand or walk on your feet, or get into a tub of warm water. Meanwhile, start correcting your dietary deficiency – the amount of calcium you need to take depends on individual results – and you will soon be delivered of the cramps.

Smoking

As you know, smoking has been found medically to be a definite cause of lung cancer. But there are other hazards you may not know of. Smoking can also lead to faster ageing. Smoking has even led to heart attacks, not only in smokers themselves, but in those toward whom smokers blow their smoke! Researchers have found also that smoking definitely causes facial wrinkles. It may be a matter of time, but if you continue smoking, those wrinkles will come.

Some people smoke because they are shy, nervous, insecure, or under stress. They may also be victims of hypoglycemia, due to dietary lack of protein and B vitamins, as well as too many sweets.

I will share with you a method Captain William P. Knowles (mentioned in the chapter on breathing) has developed. He says that of his students, from a hundred countries, eight out of ten have stopped smoking entirely or greatly reduced their intake by this method. One secretary, who smoked twenty-five cigarettes daily and had suffered from bronchitis and a cough, stopped smoking in two months. Later she tried a cigarette to test herself. She said the taste was awful. Her desire to smoke had disappeared, together with the bronchitis and the cough.

Here is Captain Knowles's method for stopping the smoking habit. It is done three times daily for three minutes each time.

1. Sit upright in a chair. Do not touch the back of the chair with your spine.
2. Stretch your arms forward, then draw them back slowly; let your elbows rest against the sides of your body; put hands, palms down, on your thighs.
3. Breathe in and out quickly through your nose about a dozen times. A smoker may cough and sputter, but this is good for expelling phlegm and stale air.
4. Once the lungs are cleansed, exhale slowly and completely until there is no air left in your lungs. Then inhale to the count of seven. Pause for one second, then exhale. Do this breathing fourteen times, seven in and seven out. Keep your chest out and shoulders back to allow freedom for breathing. That's it!

Constipation

People spend more time worrying about constipation than necessary. It is easily conquered once you learn how. Laxatives are not the answer for two reasons: They flush out of the body your water soluble vitamin/mineral intake by drawing on the body fluids to produce an evacuation. They are also habit forming, so that you become dependent on them.

If you have an emergency, herbal laxatives from health stores are safer than commercial products or taking *any* laxative daily. A cupful of yogurt, or a teaspoonful of whole flaxseed or powdered psyllium seed swallowed quickly with water (the seeds become gelatinous once swallowed) will usually tide you over your immediate difficulty.

My favourite is clay. There are various clays, and some are better for different purposes, some for external, others for internal use. The one I use is from France, green clay, loaded with minerals, and an effective, natural, easy remedy for constipation. You stir up one teaspoonful of it in a half-glass of water and let it sit all day or all night. (Do *not* leave the metal spoon in the glass.) In the morning, or at night, drink the water that remains at the top after the clay has settled. Depending upon your needs, take it either before breakfast or before bedtime (it works about eight hours later), or, as many people do, take it both times. It also acts as a detoxifier and gives you many added benefits.

The most popular constipation remedy at the present time is a high-fibre diet. This means plenty of fresh raw fruits and vegetables. Or, if it agrees with you, you can take bran. The bran should not be rough and scratchy, but in softer flake form. Taken together with plenty of water, bran swells to provide bulk, and doctors and laymen are happy with the results. You can take a teaspoonful as a starter for a few days and then increase as necessary. It can also be sprinkled over cereals, raw or cooked. At my house I make my own bran muffins. Here is the recipe. They are excellent for breakfast. Everybody likes them.

Bran Muffins
Mixture One
In a bowl combine:
1 cupful unbleached flour
1 cupful bran flakes (from health store)
3 teaspoonsful baking powder
1 cupful blueberries, fresh or frozen, or other fruit of your choice. Or you may use raisins or chopped dates, plus spices. Experiment with variations. (Choose any amount you wish.)

Mixture Two
In a blender, or other container, combine:
1 cupful milk
Honey to taste (I use approximately $\frac{1}{4}$ cupful)
1 egg
3 tablespoonsful oil

Stir each mixture well and separately, then combine the two. Stir, do not beat, until the batter is well blended. It should be stiff. If not, add more bran, or flour, or both. Drop by spoonsful into a greased muffin pan, or crinkled paper cups inserted into pan (to avoid scrubbing the pan afterward). Bake at 400°F (204°C, Gas mark 6) until lightly brown (about thirty minutes). Makes a dozen muffins.

Eat one or two daily, according to your needs. Leftovers can be moistened and reheated in a slightly warm oven. Or they can be split and toasted.

Insomnia

There is nothing more aggravating than not being able to sleep. But sleeping pills are NOT the answer. They can become habit forming and are also potentialy dangerous. Combined with alcohol they can be as fatal as if you gulped down too many. Why take a chance when there are easier, safer methods?

Adelle Davis recommended keeping calcium (lactate) tablets on your bedside table. She called them lullaby pills. She said if you need more during the night take them. They are harmless.

Personally, I keep on my bedside table something I like better: the small homoeopathic specific cell salt tablets for such problems. You dissolve them dry on the tongue. If you cannot sleep, take approximately a teaspoonful of these tiny tablets, and they will soon send you to dreamland. They are called Nerve Tonic Tablets, are available at health shops and absolutely safe and are not habit-forming.

Getting more exercise daily may help you sleep better at night. Outdoor workers rarely suffer from insomnia.

What you eat before you go to bed influences your sleeping too. Often the later you eat before bedtime, the harder you will find it to sleep restfully, without tossing, turning, and bad dreams. Adelle Davis always recommended a large breakfast, a medium lunch, and a light 'supper'. This was found to promote better sleeping, as proved by a study done in a California prison back in the 1930s. This study found that the more protein taken just before bedtime, the greater the sleep disturbance. Fats or carbohydrates seemed preferable, and eating less or nothing at all near bedtime produced the least restlessness of all. However, some people who eat lightly or not at all in the evening may wake up hungry in the middle of the night, so use your own judgement.

Certain types of mild exercise taken just before bedtime can help overcome insomnia. One doctor, Edmund Jacobsen, M.D., a relaxation specialist, suggests relaxing your eye and throat muscles as you go to sleep. He has found that this hastens sleep more quickly than relaxing any other part of your body. Another doctor, M.N. Pai, recommends our Muscle Massage technique, described in Chapter 13, to induce all-over body relaxation.

Try counting your blessings instead of sheep, and if you simply cannot sleep, do not just lie there; get up and do a boring chore until you do feel sleepy.

Although eight hours of sleep have been recommended for the average person, this may or may not apply to everybody. There has been some speculation that the older a person becomes, the less sleep is needed. The Russians, supported by their scientific research in this area, refute this, believing that one hour of sleep for every three of the twenty-four-hour day — or eight hours — can regenerate cells and metabolism, particularly of the ageing individual. Without this amount of sleep they believe that normal, daily activity can destroy the cells and metabolism faster than they can be rebuilt.

As proof they cite the well-documented dog study. An old dog had lost all of his teeth, and his coat sadly lacked the lustre of youth. He was checked continuously during a three-months' experiment in rejuvenation by a staff of doctors and technicians in the laboratory. During this time the dog was kept asleep, by means of a harmless drug, twenty-three out of twenty-four hours daily and was given vitamins, minerals, proteins, and other food supplements in concentrated form by intravenous injections. After the sixth week a change took place in the dog. His coat became soft and glossy, and he appeared younger. At the end of twelve weeks (the end of the experiment) he was playing like a puppy and looking and acting young.

Even though man's life span is six times longer than a dog's, and it might take man six times longer for similar rejuvenation, the experimenters believe that through extra sleep, as well as extra nutrients, cells are rebuilt and metabolism is restimulated faster than activity could destroy them. (This study was conducted by Baines at the Davidovsky Laboratory, U.S.S.R. Psychiatry Institute, in 1957.)

Overweight and Fasting
I have written a small book on this problem. It is called *Be Slim and Healthy*, and it has all of the safe answers for reducing. A recent tip: When you discover that most carbohydrates are the weight-makers, do NOT avoid fresh fruits. They are high in carbohydrates, but you can lose weight on them because they contain enzymes. (This information arrived after I had finished the book.) Otherwise, everything you want to know about losing weight safely, without hunger and without fasting (which I disapprove of), is included in the book just mentioned. It is in paperback at health stores.

Acid-Alkaline Balance
This subject is so greatly misunderstood that I have refused to tackle it before. Some foods, which seem to be acid, produce in your body an alkaline reaction, and some foods and vegetables, which seem to be nonacid, produce acid. It is very confusing. Let's simplify it once and for all. Citrus fruits, which taste like acid, actually can produce alkalinity. Lemon juice is less of a problem. Since it is so sour, most people do not take too much of it. But people who guzzle orange or grapefruit juice think they are doing themselves a favour, partly because they are told these juices contain vitamin C. You have to drink a lot of these juices to get the amount of vitamin C in one 250 or 500mg tablet. Vitamin C or apple cider vinegar can provide acid in a helpful form. Judge Tom R. Blaine, an author on allergies says: 'Taking excessive amounts of citrus and other juices over a long period of time may produce an alkalyzed system, indicated by nasal [and anal] itching, as well as headaches, restlessness, and inability to sleep.'

Most people need more acid-promoting foods than alkaline foods. Just remember this: *A germ cannot live in an acid medium.* In the laboratory germs are grown in an alkaline medium, which may be sugars or other forms of alkalinity. But they are killed by acid.

Sometimes, if you find yourself feeling very weary or prone to any germ that comes along, try some apple cider vinegar in water and sip it with your meals (or between meals) like wine. You will feel a pickup in minutes. It is similar to turning on the electricity that lights up the room. Acid apparently generates body electricity. Make your own apple vinegar mixture to taste pleasant, and see for yourself. It mixes well with honey.

Alcohol
Avoid hard drink. I have covered this subject thoroughly in my *Handbook of Natural Remedies for Common Ailments*, so I will not repeat it here. Suffice to say that Seniors who do not have anything pleasant to look forward to may often enjoy a glass of dry wine (preferably red) just prior to, or with, the evening meal. No more! You can become a 'wino' as easily as a hard-drinking alcoholic, so use this treat according to the rules instead of abusing it.

Teeth and Gums
One problem that plagues Seniors is diminishing or weakening teeth, as well as gum afflictions. There is a nutritional remedy for these problems, and the sooner you begin, the quicker the results. The remedies are nutritional, and need time to be built into your body. They work well, but are not instantaneous.

Calcium is an integral part of our bones and teeth. If we do not get enough calcium, then one part of the body borrows it from another part, often from the teeth, causing cavities. Also, as we have said before, there may be a sufficient calcium intake, but if there is insufficient acid to digest it, the calcium merely piles up in unwanted places without doing the job it is supposed to do.

Seniors who develop loose teeth will be cheered by a study conducted by two Cornell University researchers. When 1,000mg of calcium gluconate or calcium carbonate were given patients *on a daily basis for six months*, X-rays showed that fresh bone had appeared in the jaw bones (which hold teeth firm).[2]

Bone meal, especially raw bone meal, is particularly helpful in rebuilding bones, preventing or speeding the healing of fractures, sometimes arresting cavities, even repairing them in some cases and *preventing fractures*. (Seniors are prone to fractures.) I fed my mother bone meal every day of her life from age sixty on until she died at eighty-seven. She did no suffer a single fracture, although many of her contemporaries did. (Bone meal is available at health stores in tablet or powdered form.)

As for gum disturbances, vitamin C, as well as Bioflavonoids (the entire C complex or family), firms up gums and prevents or heals weak and bleeding gums.

Appearance

There is no reason for Seniors to look unattractive. You can be attractive at any age, and you should be, to give others as well as yourself pleasure. No one likes to see a droopy, unpleasant-looking person.

As an example, a true story recently appeared in a newspaper of a woman who decided to test this idea. She wore her worst-looking jeans, left off her makeup, and let her hair become tousled and uncombed. Attired in the most unattractive way possible, she entered a bank and asked to cash a cheque. The bank refused, saying she did not have an account there. She was treated coolly and without respect.

Next she went to a good restaurant and asked for a table. She was hastily hidden behind a large plant, where she waited while forty other customers, though they came in later than she, were seated ahead of her.

Next she went to an expensive dress shop and was told she could not try on dresses unless she was clean.

Two days later the same woman, her hair well groomed, her make-up artfully applied, and her clothes neat and attractive, went into the same bank, asked to cash another cheque and got the cash immediately.

In the same restaurant as before she was promptly given an excellent table. And at the same dress shop as before she was encouraged to try on their most expensive dresses.

So looks count!

And a Note of Advice to Grown Children and Well-meaning Friends

Today it is rare to find a younger person, particularly in the early and later teenage group, who would relish being seen conversing with an older adult. Listen to the elders. Let them talk, at least *try* to be interested in their problems and interests. And don't be condescending. Treat them normally, not like children.

And for those grown children who have elderly friends or parents, do not drop in on them without warning. No one in the older age group wants to be embarrassed by being caught without such props as contact lenses (they may not be able to see you well), or a hearing aid (they may not hear what you are saying), or their false teeth (without which they may appear frightening). You may say, 'How silly, why let a little thing like that upset you?' Don't judge prematurely. Most of us want to put our best face forward. Wait until you are your parent's age. Don't judge glibly or thoughtlessly. Most people are very sensitive about not appearing 'normal'.

One friend's husband had had his leg amputated below the knee. He has an artificial leg, but like other artificial spare parts, even false teeth, it is often very uncomfortable to wear these substitutes hour in, hour out. This man, when he had donned his new leg and put on his trousers, after long, hard, painful hours of adjusting to it, had learned to walk so well that few people knew of his handicap. Yet at home, when only his wife is present, due to discomfort, he does not put on the device until necessary. He lives in dread of someone dropping in unannounced and catching him without his substitute leg. I unthinkingly dropped in one day without previous announcement. I heard scurrying noises behind the door after I rang the bell, then his wife answered the door looking a bit flurried. I immediately asked for her husband, and she explained with embarrassment that he was in the other room hastily putting on his artificial leg.

With older people in particular thoughtfulness goes a long way in helping them see – and thus feel – themselves in the best light.

REFERENCES
(See *Bibliography* for fuller details.)

1. Anna Kaye, with Don C. Matchan, Reflexology: Techniques of Foot Massage for Health and Fitness.
2. Linda Clark, *Know Your Nutrition*.

17

Your Rejuvenation Blueprint

A Summary

1. You need to rebuild your body by rebuilding your cells. This is done mainly by feeding your cells the best fuel available. Although vitamins and minerals are important, you need, first and foremost, the right kind of food. Introduce the high-powered foods, mentioned in Chapter 11, gradually into your diet. This provides your health foundation. Then add vitamin/mineral supplements as needed. Read *Know Your Nutrition* to learn which ones they are. Be sure to eat plenty of raw foods and sprouts. Eat less, chew more.

Good health does not come instantly, but you will notice it on a good day now and then after you embark on your new programme. The good days gradually increase until they are the rule, not the exception.

2. Find the exercise that appeals to you and do it daily. Be sure to do your breathing exercises too.

3. Watch your thinking. Set up your blueprint according to how you want to feel, look, and act. Follow through, no matter what temptation arises, until good thinking becomes a habit.

4. Radiate love to everyone, and your inner beauty (or handsomeness, if you are a man) will take care of itself.

5. Improve your appearance. You have been given hints of how to do this all through the book.

Meanwhile, don't stoop when you stand, sit, or walk. Stand tall like royalty! The best exercise I know for becoming erect is the one I have often talked of and was invented by a young girl who had miserable posture, as well as a spinal curvature. This exercise not only led to her being used as a model on the Liberty quarter (at the beginning of World War I), but overcame her spinal curvature, as confirmed by a physician. Here are the directions for the exercise:

Put your hands behind your back, arms straight, hands back to back. Interlace the backs of the fingers of both hands. Now twist your thumbs, first toward your spine, then away from it. Repeat often. It straightens your spine, raises your chest, and pulls in your stomach.

When you walk, do not give away your age by shuffling. Stride, swinging your legs from your hips, your arms from the shoulders.

You can't look well if you don't feel well. A five-year study of seven thousand California residents was conducted by researchers at the University of California. Richard Passwater, nutrition writer, reports: 'They studied seven health habits and found that people who get adequate sleep, eat breakfast, stay lean, avoid empty calorie snacks (pastries, pop, sweets, biscuits), don't smoke, exercise regularly, and either don't drink or take very little alcohol are rewarded with superior health. ... Those who followed all the good practices were in better health at every age than those who only followed one or few.' In other words, you must programme your rejuvenation, not leave it to chance.

Another example: One woman, a great-grandmother, refused to act her age. Instead of knitting or gossiping, she took up basketball, swimming, and bowling. Adding good nutrition and good thinking to such a programme will make you a winner!

So influence the years you live, don't let the years you live influence you.

And if anyone asks you how you are, don't whine, 'Pretty well.' Stand up straight, look the other person straight in the eye, and even if you temporarily feel like falling over, say firmly, 'FINE!' Like a strong, instead of a fishy, handshake, that should get the message across to everybody, including your subconscious, that whatever your age, you mean success.

Appoint yourself a committee of one to start reversing the poor image of Seniors. Help us all to make the most of our potential so that we can be proud of ourselves and our group. *Start Now*.

I hope this information in this book will add happy years to your life. Forget your age and make the most of your years, which should be the best part of your life. Make them so!

18

Rejuvenation From Tibet

I have saved the most exciting method of rejuvenation for the last. In 1975 I was introduced to a chemical engineer. He knew of my work and told me he had come across a method of rejuvenation that might interest me in a book he had called the *Five Rites of Rejuvenation*. This book tells an amazing story.

It concerns an elderly, retired British army colonel who looked, felt, and acted old. When he had been stationed in India, some natives had told him of a lamasery, where the lamas had discovered the secret of youth. In this group there were no people who looked, felt, or acted old.

After a long, exhaustive search he finally found the group and asked to be taught the technique. When he first arrived, he was called 'The Ancient One'. But after a month on the technique he no longer looked ancient. When he first saw himself in a mirror, he could not believe the change, and when he returned to England no one recognized him – except those who thought he was his son!

The colonel explained the method to a friend, telling him it had been kept secret for centuries. The technique he was taught is explained in the book, and I shall give it here.

The body has seven magnetic centres, called vortexes. In a healthy body they revolve at great speed; when they slow down, ill health, old age, senility appear.

These vortexes are located as follows: two in the brain; one at the base of the throat; one in the right side above the waist line; one in the reproductive anatomy; and one in each knee.

These spinning centres of activity extend beyond the flesh in the healthy individual, but not in the old, weak, or senile person. The quickest way to regain health, youth, and vitality is to start these magnetic centres spinning again.

There are five exercises. Any one will be helpful, but all five are required to get glowing results. The lamas call them Rites, instead of exercises.

After the colonel achieved his own rejuvenation in India, he returned to England and started small classes in which he taught the Rites. He refused to enrol any person under fifty years old. Every single student reported improvement. One of them, a man close to seventy-five, made especially remarkable progress.

The five Rites are practised once each three times daily to start, and increased to twenty-one times daily. All five Rites require only a few minutes. One day a week can be missed, but no more. The booklet states that improvement continues even after two years, when a still more pronounced change in appearance and condition is possible.

Both men and women can do them. My chemical engineer acquaintance told me he had practised them himself for two years. I had never seen him before, but at sixty he looks closer to forty-five. Another man told me that he had practised the Rites for six years with nothing but highly satisfactory results, although he did indicate that good nutrition was also necessary. This man now practises the Rites only ten times a day. If you cannot keep up the twenty-one times, settle for as many as seem comfortable for you.

The Rites are not really difficult, although you have to get used to some of them. Stiffness may interfere initially, but this soon passes. The whirling exercise, should be taken carefully at first. If you get dizzy, STOP, sit down, and wait until the next session to try it again. Eventually you will find that the longer you work at the Rites, the easier they become.

In the pages that follow I shall give a description of the five Rites, accompanied by an illustration of each

Rite No. 1

Stand erect, arms outstretched, horizontal with the shoulders. Now turn around in a *clockwise direction* only. Fasten your eyes on a starting point and count rotations as you return to this spot. At first, practice this Rite only to the point of slight dizziness. As time passes and your vortexes revolve more rapidly, you will be able to repeat the Rite more often with less discomfort. Take it ease.

Lie full length on the floor. Place your arms, palms flat on the floor, alongside your hips. Raise you feet until your legs are straight up. If possible, let them extend lightly beyond your head, but do not bent your knees. Then slowly lower your legs to the floor, relax and repeat.

Rite No. 2

One of the lamas found when he began this exercise that he was so old, weak, and decrepit he could not possibly lift both legs. With bent knees at first, he lifted his thighs, letting his feet hang down. Little by little he could straighten his legs. By the end of the third month he could lift them straight up with ease.

Rite No 3.

Kneel on the floor, place your hands on your thighs and lean as far forward as possible, with your chin resting on your chest.

Now lean backward as far as possible, also leaning the head backward as far as it will go.

Bring your head upright, body straight, to starting position. Repeat the Rite.

Rite No. 4

This seems hard at first, but after a week becomes surprisingly easy. Sit on the floor, feet and legs outstretched in front of you. Place your hands palms down, arms straight directly under your shoulders, against your body. Put your head or chin on your chest.

Now bend your knees, feet flat on the floor, and raise your body until it makes a table. Let your head drop gently backward as far as it will go. Return to a sitting position, then repeat. If you cannot get the 'feel' of it, do not become discouraged. You might lie on a low box at first until you can eventually push your body to a table position without a prop.

Rite No. 5

Place your hands, palms down, on the floor. Kneel on your knees, and then stretch your body upward until your hips are as high as possible. Head should be down and forward.

Slowly lower your hips until your body sags. Let your head bend back as far as possible. Return to a knee position and repeat.

Some Rites are harder for some, whereas others are harder for others. Rites No. 4 and 5 are more difficult for most people.

REJUVENATION FROM TIBET

But do the ones you can, and try the others until you become proficient in all. Sooner or later your muscles will become strong, and you will be able to do them all with ease.

These Rites can be practised morning or night, or both. But because they are stimulating, morning might be best.

Three times a day for the first week is recommended. Then increase them by two a day until you are doing twenty-one a day, which will be the beginning of the tenth week.

If you cannot do the whirling Rite, number one, the same number of times as the others, do it only as many times as you can without getting too dizzy. Eventually you will be able to do it the same number of times as the others. If you have had any injury or operation, wait until you are well before beginning them (ask your doctor).

Suggested Reading

Chapman, J.B., M.D., edited by Cogswell, J.W., M.D., *Dr Schuessler's Biochemistry*. Thorsons Publishers Limited.

Clark, Linda, *Be Slim and Healthy*. New Canaan, Conn.: Keats Publishing Company, 1972*

——, *Face Improvement through Exercise and Nutrition*. New Canaan, Conn.: Keats Publishing Company*

——, *A Handbook of Natural Remedies for Common Ailments*. Wellingborough, Northants.: Thorsons Publishers Limited, 1980.

——, *Secrets of Health and Beauty*. Old Greenwich, Conn.: The Devin-Adair Company, 1969; New York: Pyramid Books, 1971, paperback*

——, *Stay Young Longer*. New York: Pyramid Books, 1968, paperback*

——, *The Best of Linda Clark* (an anthology). New Canaan, Conn.: Keats Publishing Company, 1976*

——, with Karen Kelly, *Beauty Questions and Answers*. New York: Pyramid Books, 1977

——, with Yvonne Martine, *Health, Youth and Beauty through Color Breathing*. Millbrae, Calif.: Celestial Arts*

Cornaro, Luigi, *How to Live 100 Years*. Wellingborough, Northants.: Thorsons Publishers Ltd., 1978

Davis, Adelle, *Let's Eat Right to Keep Fit*. Pondon: Allen and Unwin 1971.

Kaye, Anna, with Don C. Matchan, *Reflexology: Techniques of Foot Massage for Health and Fitness*. Wellingborough, Northants.: Thorsons Publishers, 1979

Silva, José, and Miele, Philip, *The Silva Mind Control Method*. London: Souvenir Press 1978

Stephenson, James R., M.D., *A Doctor's Guide to Helping*

Yourself with Homoeopathic Remedies. Wellingborough: Thorsons Publishers Limited, Northants.

Williams, Roger J., *Biochemical Individuality*. New York: Wiley, 1956; now available in paperback from the University of Texas Press

——, *You are Extraordinary*. New York: Berkely Jove

---

* UK Distributors: Thorsons Publishers Limited, Wellingborough, Northants.

Index

acid-alkaline balance, 109-10
acidophilus, 66
Adams, Rex, 70
alcohol, 41, 48, 110
Allen, Mary, 47
amino acids, 51
amylase, 40
angina, 28, 33-4
appearance, 111
artery, clogging of, 28
  problems, 27-8
arteriosclerosis, 27
Arbus, Louis, 75
arthritis, 34, 35
atherosclerosis, 27
'auxin' foods, 62, 63

birth defects, causes of, 13
Blaine, Tom R., 109
Bloodworth, Dr Venice, 100
Bock, Raymond F., 73
bran muffins, recipe for, 106-7
breathing techniques, 91-5
brewer's yeast, 49, 64
Burroughs, Stanley A., 57-9

calcium, 103-4
  deposits, 29
  treating, 34
Carrel, Alexis, 17, 18, 54
cells, 18
  loss of with ageing, 16-18
  regeneration of, 17
  therapy (Niehans treatment), 54, 55
cholesterol, 29-35
  clogging of arteries by, 29-31
  dissolving, 32-5
Christopher, John R., 59
chymotrypsin, 40
cleansing programme, 57-9
constipation, 105-7
Coupan, Paul, 75
Cropp, Caroline, 56, 59-60

Davis, Adelle, 50, 107
death, fear of, 11-12
degenerative diseases, 25-6, 27-47
De Vries, Herbert, 80
digestion, 47
  use of enzymes for, 36-42
Duche, George, 75

Eck, Paul, 47
eggs, 63
  and cholesterol, 29-30
enzymes, 36-42, 50
exercise, 80-90
  internal, 87, 88
  T'ai Chi, 88, 89
  Tibetan Rites, 116-23
  Yoga, 89-90

fasting, 57-9, 109
fats, 32, 33, 40, 41
feet, and bodily health, 102, 103
  care of, 103
'flu, 68
Froimovich, Jose, 15, 18

garlic, 69-70
gamma globulin, 67
glands, 20-22, 45-52, 54-7
  and ageing, 20-21

INDEX

concentrates for menopause and prostate, 60, 61
effect of on health, 13-15

HCL (hydrochloric acid), 39-40, 48
herbs, 59
Hewitt, Edward, 67
Hill, Caryl, 92
homoeopathy, 24, 76, 79
Howell, Edward, 41, 42, 47, 62
Huang, Teh, 30
Hungerford, Mary Jane, 51

insomnia, 107-8

Jacobson, Edmund, 108
Jarvis, D.C., 34

Kakiashvili, David, 83
Kaye, Anna, 87
Kelley, Dr William, 32, 47
Knowles, Capt. N.P., 91, 92
Kubler-Ross, Elisabeth, 11-12
Kugler, Hans J., 17

lactase, 36
Landone, Brown, 62
Leaf, Alexander, 72
lecithin, 32-4, 67-9
Lee, Dr Royal, 32
leg cramps, 103, 104
'life force', 86, 87
Longevity Research Institute, 28, 29, 33

Matchan, Don C. 87
memory, improving, 75, 76
  loss of, 18, 19
milk intolerance, 36, 37
minerals, 61, 72
Morrison, Lester M., 32, 67, 68
muscle massage exercise, 83-5
Myers, John A., 72

negative ionizers (air cleansers), 94-5
Niehans, Paul, 54, 55, 60, 61
Nittler, Alan, 68
Norton, Suza, 93

nucleic acids, 74
nutrition, 25-6

overweight, 109
oxygen, 17, 18, 19, 64, 65, 66, 83, 91-5

Packer, Lester, 17
Pai, M.N., 108
Passwater, Richard A., 29, 30, 33, 114
periwinkle extract, 75-6
placenta, 60
protein, 49, 50, 51, 52, 64, 69

reflexology, 87
Rinse, Jacobus, 34
Rites, Tibetan, 116-23
RNA-DNA (nucleic acids) 74
Robinson, Arthur, 47

Salt, need for, 70-71
  free diet, 70, 71
Smith, James, 17
Smith, Justa, 41
smoking, 104-5
spleen, 60
sprouts, 62, 63
Steinhaus, Arthur, 84

teeth and gums, 110-11
thymus, 60
Tibetan Rites, 116-23
trypsin, 40
Tuckey, Dr Hugh, 39

vegetarianism, 47
vinegar, cider apple, 34
vitamins, 73-4, 46
  A, 31, 38, 46
  avoiding loss of, 38
  B6, 31, 108
  B-complex, 31, 32, 73
  C, 16, 24, 31, 34, 67, 73
  D, 31, 103
  E, 16, 31, 32, 34, 73
  K, 31

Watson, George, 47

Other recommended reading...

LINDA CLARK'S HANDBOOK OF NATURAL REMEDIES
FOR COMMON AILMENTS

Linda Clark. Shows how to enjoy good health the natural way. Linda Clark is a leading reporter on health and nutrition and her book is a first-aid kit no one should be without — a thoroughly documented, easy-to-understand guide for all those who wish to take more responsibility for their own health and well-being. It covers many ailments, including allergies, anaemia, arthritis, asthma, backache, constipation, fatigue, headaches, indigestion, heart trouble and high blood pressure. In this book you will almost certainly find an effective new healing approach to whatever ails you.